Susan Fox Rogers

TWO
IN THE
WILD

A rock climber for over twenty years,
Susan Fox Rogers has edited a number
of anthologies including *Solo: On Her
Own Adventure, Alask--
Voic-- f*

Jackie

TWO
IN THE
WILD

Tales of Adventure
from Friends, Mothers,
and Daughters

●●

EDITED AND WITH AN INTRODUCTION BY

SUSAN FOX ROGERS

VINTAGE DEPARTURES

Vintage Books · A Division of Random House, Inc. · New York

A VINTAGE DEPARTURES ORIGINAL, SEPTEMBER 1999
FIRST EDITION

Library of Congress Cataloging-in-Publication Data
Two in the wild : tales of adventure from friends, mothers, and
daughters / edited by Susan Fox Rogers. — 1st ed.
p.   cm. — (Vintage departures)
ISBN 0-375-70201-6
1. Outdoor recreation for women—Literary collections.
2. Adventure stories, American—Women authors.   3. Wilderness
survival—Literary collections.   4. American prose literature—
Women authors.   5. Outdoor life—Literary collections.
I. Rogers, Susan Fox.
PS648.088T88   1999
810.8'0355—dc21   99-20934
CIP

Author photograph © Linda Smukler
Book design by Suvi Asch

www.vintagebooks.com

Printed in the United States of America
10   9   8   7   6   5   4   3   2   1

For Alice and Thomas,
the youngest adventurers in my life

ACKNOWLEDGMENTS

Anthologies are by nature group projects, but putting them together—licking the envelopes, begging for manuscripts, writing revision letters—can be a solo journey. On this one I was lucky to have Deb Jane Addis, her broken leg propped up on a chair after a rock-climbing accident, read and discuss every essay I received (hundreds). Faith Conlon and Holly Morris are at the heart of this book because they both have been pioneers in women's outdoor writing. LuAnn Walther—my first guide on the editorial path—has more to do with this book than she will ever know. Dorothy Varon provided much needed legal help. Lucy Jane Bledsoe was a catalyst in this collection's road to publication. Teri Condon yanked me out of my chair for a few real-life adventures that reminded me why I do this. My editor Dawn Davis was intrepid on this bumpy adventure, and her assistant, Adam, heroic. Sam read, counseled, soothed, and encouraged me through all the ups and downs of this process. Above all, the many women who sent their stories—whether I included them or not—inspired me with wild adventures, well told.

CONTENTS

INTRODUCTION

••

Susan Fox Rogers

When I edited a collection of women's solo outdoor adventures, people often asked: isn't solo travel dangerous? Yes, it is. Traveling alone, a woman faces obvious physical dangers, and she is seen as either foolish or very brave. Foolish or not, it's something that some of us need, like air or water. We balance the dangers.

With this collection of essays about women traveling together into the outdoors in pairs, my guess is I won't be asked that same question. But at the moment I'm picturing Thelma and Louise leaving behind their no-good men and lighting out for the West. With gas in the tank and the sun high, anything could happen. There's danger in their laughter and freedom. There's exhilaration in their power. Yes, there's risk in traveling in duos, only the stakes are different.

The bonds formed while hiking into the desert are not the ones created at the water cooler or over an arugula salad lunch. When we sweat and struggle together, trust each other on the end of a rope, something remarkable develops. Love, complex and strong, is what we often hope for—our expectations of sisterly bonding are high. But the opposite can just as easily happen. In the quest for the ideal adventure a long list of issues emerges: trust, sexuality, competition. Things don't always go as planned, and what results can be more exciting—or more complicated. But what better place to let the unexpected happen than under an ocean sky or on a snow-covered bowl at 12,000 feet?

Most of the essays gathered here describe adventures with friends, as in Sara Corbett's high-jinks ride through Australia's outback with Sugar, who is as richly described as her name. These friends become rebels, foot heavy on the gas pedal, pushing the limits of where we are "supposed" to go as women, who we are "supposed" to be. When the dust settles what remains is what we all hope for: a friendship as wide as the Australian sky, built on laughter and shared mishaps.

Something about movement, or maybe just mountain air, allows for intimacy. After great loss, Pam Houston is willing to let a friend into her life during a Colorado spring thaw. And though the extent of their physical challenge is tossing rocks into a stream, the bonding that occurs during a gift of free time outdoors is one that surprises Houston. The physical energy between two women can also ignite into love—as it does in BK Loren's poetic essay about the beginning of her relationship with her lover. Or that energy can tear at a friendship—as it does for Lea Aschkenas hiking in Chile. Either way, the situation can be volatile.

Not all these adventures involve established friendships. Lucy Jane Bledsoe encounters a woman riding her bike across the desert, and the woman's extreme situation—fleeing an abusive husband—leads Bledsoe to reflect on the history and meaning of the bicycle, both in her own life and in the lives of all women. In one case, only the spirit of another woman is present. Amy Irvine hikes into the Tetons with thoughts of Amy Bechtel, a runner who had tragically disappeared a year earlier. Irvine's meditations on safety are ones we as women must consider, but they are made more immediate through the spiritual connection that the writer forms with the missing Amy.

One of the strongest duo bonds is that of mother and daughter, and several writers here explore the strength and complexity of adventures that involve muscle, emotions, and blood ties. Hannah Nyala takes her young daughter for a desert backpacking trip to heal their past and the two years they have been apart. Kathleen Dean Moore takes a boat trip in Alaska with her daughter, who is no longer the child who needs to be taken care of, no longer the one who needs to be taught.

As all these essays reveal, the bonds created on a bike or in the snow can be stronger than love itself—or far from perfect. What these writers have been able to show is the intricacy of our intimate lives as we venture forth. Here there is love, but little romance. And always these tales are set in beautiful and wondrous places: Tibet, Costa Rica, the Pacific Northwest, Colorado, Australia, Alaska. The adventures undertaken range from fly-fishing to roadtripping, backcountry skiing to mountain biking, cowboying to backpacking. With sweat and guts, all of these essays will take you on a physical or emotional journey that will be fun or unexpected, tender or hilarious. Enjoy.

TWO IN THE WILD

IS THAT A WALLABY IN YOUR POCKET?

●●

Sara Corbett

THE LONG NIGHT OF SUICIDAL BOOMERS

Not one day into the outback and we're breaking the no-driving-at-sunset rule. It's sunset and, sure as shoot, we're driving. My friend Sugar has the wheel and is doing in the neighborhood of eighty miles an hour on the gravel road, creating a cyclone of rat-a-tooing rock beneath our floorboards. It feels like someone's firing an assault rifle at the underbelly of the car, a Subaru station wagon that doesn't belong to us. I'm sunk deep in the passenger's seat, expecting one shot will hit the bull's-eye and detonate our gas tank. Sugar solves the problem by boosting the stereo volume another notch and belting out a Lena Horne tune: "This is a fine romance. This is a fine roMANCE!" She is just shy of six feet tall, Sugar is, with white blond hair and the kind of complexion women try to buy. She works the gas pedal with a size-ten foot. When we first met, we were fifteen years old. Just recently, for better or worse, we turned thirty. The sky ahead of us is so big and purple that the land itself, a buckled, darkening plane of dry earth and scrub grass, seems incidental.

This is the hour we've been warned about: that dusky, confused time when kangaroos emerge in squads from the bushes to make fatal leaps at the rare passing car. Kangaroo suicide hour. Mick, the wizened tractor driver we met at the gas station a few hours back, said, "They'll bloody wreck ya. Hit a 'roo and I reckon ya walk the rest of the way to Alice Springs. On crutches."

We know so little. We left the wine bars and botanical gardens of Adelaide, the coastal capital of South Australia, six hours ago, traveling a strip-malled highway that gave way to rolling country road and crumbled finally into this deserted, rubbly boulevard. For the last hour we've been shotgunning north through a colorless limestone prairie that looks like something that's been left in the oven too long. The maps detailing our route all look the same: desert to the left, desert to the right, and a dotted red line that ticks its way up through the outback. "Outback" is Australian for "out back of the bloody beyond." I read this in a guidebook, the same place I read that we definitely should not be driving at sunset, and that Australia is home to the world's most venomous snakes— king snakes, tiger snakes, brown snakes, and something called the desert death adder. Sugar happily eschews any third-party input, guidebooks and maps included. "I like to be surprised," is what she says.

Prior to meeting in Adelaide last night, we'd let ten years slip by without a visit. We postcarded through our twenties, writing sporadic three-by-five editorials on our go-nowhere jobs, go-nowhere love affairs, trips to Africa and China, graduate school, abrupt cross-country moves, better jobs, better love, and still more wandering. But a month ago, staring down the barrel of my fourth decade, I suddenly got anxious to catch up with Sugar. Call me a pessimist, but another five years and I imagine phoning up out of the blue for a girls-only road trip will not be so simple.

This kind of thing gets both of us down. We are happy, privileged people, Sugar and I, yet thinking about the future—about babies and husbands, in particular—occasionally gives us vertigo. Sugar has been living in Melbourne as a Fulbright scholar. She has a real name, which is Kelly, but she's been dating a cricket player for a team in Tasmania who calls her Sugar. It fits. I approve of the Tasmanian cricket player before I've met him.

We've filled every air pocket of the car with stuff. Among other things, we're carrying socket wrenches and duct tape, WD-40, two first-aid kits, a spare tire and a spare spare tire, a fire extinguisher, a compass, three kinds of rope, sixty gallons of emergency water, two weeks' worth of food, tents and sleeping bags, half a case of good Australian wine, Sugar's arsenal of Chanel products, a pile of CDs, and a glove compartment full of chocolate. We are prepared to survive anything. In the next week, we plan to find our way over a thousand miles of land so sun-hammered and empty, so famously inhospitable, that it's beaten back and broken down and swallowed up settlers and explorers for more than a century. Even now, tourists disappear down mine shafts, families inadvertently drive themselves into oblivion, dingoes steal babies. Some people simply leave their houses in the morning and never come back.

Even the city folk in Adelaide swap yarns about their eccentric neighbors in the bush. Already we've heard tales of a booze-swilling bronco rider named Phantom and a cave-dwelling playboy called Crocodile Harry. Far to the north there's Molly Clark, champion of outback women, a senior-citizen homesteader who can blow off the head of a king snake with her shotgun, who can split wood faster than any guy who dares take her on, and whom we figure we might admire. "Aw, that Molly, she'll teach yuh a thing'r two," say those who know of her, and most everyone does.

In these parts, we women are called birds. We are called chicks, chooks, and Sheilas. Sometimes, feeling respectful, the men simply call us foy-males, as in, "I reckon we don't get a lot of you *foy-males* out here in the bush." Partially for this reason, the bush is where we're taking ourselves for our Last Hurrah. Planning this trip, we had pictured ourselves as a pair of Daisy Dukes, bashing our way into the untamed heart of Australia in a two-ton monster vehicle. But the station wagon's a fine car—royal blue, spring-loaded—and we got it loaned to us for free.

"We're like two soccer moms," I say.

"Like two soccer moms touring hell," says Sugar, scanning the horizon. Sometimes we feel too old to be one thing and too young to be another.

She expertly steers around a dead kangaroo without missing a beat in her song. Every mile out here, it's another furry mountain. The live ones, some of them six feet tall, are massing silently in the indigo light, in ghostly clumps of two or three. Kangaroos are also called boomers in Australia. They have disarming deer faces, little *T. rex* arms, and the glutes of a power lifter. Some have pouches but no babies. Two hours ago they were cute. Not anymore. If the kangaroos are on the right side of the road, they appear to be gazing wistfully at the bushes on the left—and vice versa, giving the impression that at any moment they might bazooka themselves directly into our path. I am antsy. The sky is rolling into black. Sugar sings on: "We should be like a couple of hot TOMATOES, but you're as cold as yesterday's mashed POTATOES!"—and the car chatters ahead, forging two sodium pools of light on the dark, dark road.

ON YOU, ON ME, *ENNUI*

I wake with red dirt in my mouth. Red dirt in my hair and beneath my fingernails. The outback is two million square miles of mostly red dirt—bulldust, the locals call it—an iron-tasting cinnamon silt that floats off the desert dunes and coats everything, especially newcomers. Sugar, too, has been bulldusted. She has to unload the entire car before recovering our jumbo canister of Wet Ones. We mop some of the baked earth from our bodies, boil water for tea, stuff everything back into the Subaru, and start driving again.

We're following part of the Oodnadatta Track, a 400-mile dirt road that bends its way north through the deep space of south-central Australia, connecting the few places where groundwater has forced its way through the callused bedrock to create life-sustaining springs. For thousands of years the Oodnadatta was trekked by Aborigines, who traded tools for shell, ocher for boomerangs, following the invisible song lines of their ancestors. In the mid-1800s Scottish explorer John McDouall Stuart used the springs along the Oodnadatta as stepping stones to the interior as he made five disastrous attempts to cross Australia south to north. On a sixth try in 1862, with eleven men and seventy-one horses, and after eighteen months, Stuart reached the northern settlement of Darwin so exhausted that he had to be lifted from his horse. "I am now reduced to a perfect skeleton," he wrote, "a mere shadow." By my estimation, we'll be just about out of gas by the time we hit the town of William Creek, which on Friday nights, we understand, has a pub full of cowboys. Somehow we see this as a challenge.

In the meantime, Sugar and I take turns yelling stories at each other. We spent our glory years stuck together at a New England prep school, where Sugar wore frosted blue eyeliner and I had feathered hair that I cut myself. Our favorite complaint in those days was that we suffered from *ennui,* something we expressed by sweeping into other people's dorm rooms and collapsing dramatically on the couch. As far as I was concerned, it simply signified a perpetual ache for something more interesting than what we had.

All these years later, we find that we are better-adjusted versions of our old longing selves. Sugar remains a hybrid of glamour queen and Nebraska farm girl, the tall blonde in Chanel lipstick who commands an audience at the diplomat's ball, extemporizing on the merits of Caterpillar over John Deere. Before getting her Fulbright, Sugar handled education and foreign-policy issues for a prominent U.S. senator. She's thinking about running for the Senate herself someday, and I honestly believe she'll win. I live in Maine with my boyfriend and my dog in an apartment furnished with yard-sale detritus. The last time I did black-tie was with Sugar at our high-school prom, on the way to which I ripped my strapless dress right up the back, trying to scale a stone wall.

"My prom dress went to one Halloween party and got retired," says Sugar, who keeps contorting her long legs to get comfortable on the passenger's side. Twice already she's accidentally kicked the car into neutral. Her prom dress was a memorable cream-colored sateen with a starched bow the size of a sofa cushion on one hip.

"I went to my last Halloween party dressed as a mushroom," I say.

Sugar laughs the same way she always has: a big, wide-open schnort.

We pass sandy creek beds and stony creek beds; no sign of water anywhere. This part of Australia averages less than eight inches of rain a year, but when the rain does come it tends to arrive in sudden gullywashers that can fill a creek or turn a road to mush almost instantly. Not long before our arrival, one such downpour marooned twenty travelers for more than a week on a spot of high ground just north of the Oodnadatta.

Today, though, the land is a backward-moving conveyor belt of charred brown tundra. The red sun has broiled the sky white. I fish Diet Cokes and a few Tim Tams—a richer, more chocolaty version of the Oreo that's very popular in this car—from the mini-cooler we keep shoved behind the driver's seat. I read aloud from the guidebook, which says that in Aborigine culture, the land is considered a huge, detailed road map of the mind. The three people we've passed today, all in Land Cruisers and all traveling in the opposite direction, have acknowledged us by hoisting a single finger from the steering wheel, as if involving the whole hand would be too much effort. As if it hardly matters that we're all out here together.

BEFRIENDED BY MEN WITH GIANT BRAS

I find Butch, my first outback friend, slumped on a bar stool beneath a drooping 58DDD brassiere, the masterwork of a collection of bras hung like prayer flags from the rafters of the bar at the William Creek Hotel. Butch looks to be about sixty, with a weather-bitten face and an inebriate's earnestness. He wears a Cat Diesel cap and an oil-stained flannel shirt unbuttoned at the wrists, and has a hand-rolled cigarette in one hand, a beer in the other. He smells truly bad.

"Y'havin' a stubby or a tinny?" he asks, leaning in close.

"Stubby," I learn, is Australian for "beer bottle" ("bo-ohl," says Butch) and "tinny" is "beer can" ("cayrn"). Butch is nursing a tinny of XXXX. I ask for a stubby of Carlton Cold. Butch lives in a trailer some miles up the road and comes here every single night with his little dog, Muttley, a white-bellied yapper who's busy suctioning food scraps from the floor.

Out here everybody counts as a neighbor. Fly a plane over the outback at night and you'll see that humanity has made only the smallest mark—fifty or so generator-driven lights winking up from a thousand miles of darkness—and thus community knows no distance. On Friday nights, the jackaroos drive three hours across the plains to converge on the William Creek Hotel, the only building in a dusty, fly-infested town with a population of seven. Two airplanes and three Land Cruisers are parked outside, and across the street is a solar-powered pay phone, reputed to be the most remote phone booth on earth.

"Where you birds headed?" Butch wants to know, chucking his chin toward the end of the bar, where Sugar is intently studying the jukebox, her face lit yellow and purple.

I start telling Butch that we've basically got no plan—we're eyeing an opal-mining town called Coober Pedy, and after that, it's north into the bloody beyond, toward the tough granny homesteader Molly Clark. Suddenly, I've got an audience.

"Aw naw!" says one lanky man in low-slung dirty jeans and a cowboy hat. "You girls better watch yourselves in Coobah Pedy. If they don't kidnap ya, they'll bomb ya. She's a strange-ass town, that one."

"Goin' to see Molly!" booms Butch. "Chroist! She's bloody far north."

"I'd watch out for the roads," says a crinkly-eyed redhead named Tim Byrnes. "What are ya drivin'?"

I try to look nonchalant as I tell him. There are tattoos snaking up his arms.

Over the next two stubbies, I receive an onslaught of driving advice, some cautionary words about reptiles, plus three offers of personal escorts to Alice Springs. Twice I'm asked why I'm not married. Somebody wants to show me his bullwhip. After a while, it occurs to me that I've lost Sugar. Maybe she's gone to bed. I climb off my stool and take a wobbly walk around the room, shouldering through thickets of lonesome cowboys. I ask for the ladies room and am told there is none. Tim has been at my elbow for an hour, narrating every ditch and chuckhole from here to Coober Pedy. Now he wants to point out something on a map tacked to the far wall. We are halfway there when a big loud shriek—"Oh, baby!"—tells me everything I need to know: Sugar is alive and well and playing pool.

In the back room, with nine stupefied local boys watching, Sugar has cleaned up on four games straight. Sinking her last eight ball, she drags me back to the bar. "These guys are so friendly!" she says, and I don't disagree. We share some tequila with two red-cheeked jackaroos from Anna Creek. One's hat is black, the other's is gray. We learn that they work six days a week mustering cattle from one water hole to the next, for which they earn about $200. They ride motorbikes, not horses. Aside from Friday nights at the pub, they spend their evenings sitting around the homestead, watching one of two television channels they can get via satellite. They like *The X-Files* and *King of the Hill* and a whole lot of footy, which is Australian for rugby.

"It's a lonely loif," says the dark-hatted one. They are sweet and sincere. They want to get married and manage cattle stations of their own someday. When we ask, they tell us they are seventeen and twenty-three.

"Good Lord," Sugar says, pointing at the younger one. "We're like twice your age!"

"Where are you guys going to meet your wives?" I ask.

"Royt here, we reckon," the older one says solemnly.

More time passes. More tequila. I play one game of pool and give up. I've lost Sugar again. The wind is whistling through the walls. Hank Williams lows from the jukebox. The black-hatted jackaroo keeps wanting to dance. I go looking for Sugar, figuring she'll tell me whether it's a good idea or a bad idea to waltz with a jackaroo. It's late now, and there's something ultimately heart-breaking about this bush-country brotherhood—these men who call one another mate, boozing beneath a canopy of swaying bras, waiting for a wife to walk through the door. When I ask Sugar about the dancing, I know she'll say it's OK. That's what we do for each other, I realize. Then somebody points me toward her. Sugar is outside, across the street in the planet's most remote phone booth, drunk-dialing the Tasmanian cricket player under a wet moon. I cross the street and get in line.

IN THE CAVE OF 1,000 WILLING VIRGINS

If a place can feel instantly sinister, we've found it. Coober Pedy is wrecked and postapocalyptic. There are no people—except on the danger signs everywhere, warning of abandoned mine shafts, which number in the hundreds of thousands and are left uncov-ered. The signs depict black stick figures in graphic free fall. They say, DON'T RUN, DON'T WALK BACKWARD, BEWARE! In the distance we can see pyramids of spooky white gypsum, refuse piles left by excavating machines, dotting the vast opal fields like a giant, sprawling tent village.

"Weird," I say to Sugar.

"Weird," she says back. Sugar has been a slave to my hangover all day. On the rutted road from William Creek, she gently fed me

Gatorade and cucumber sandwiches. She played her disco compilation CD until I ordered her to pull over so I could spend twenty minutes sitting woozily by the side of the road. Sugar herself woke up fresh as a daisy, scarfed down a big plate of scrambled eggs, and then did all the driving. I love her and hate her for this.

It was the Aborigines who named Coober Pedy, which translates fittingly as "white man in a hole." Most of the town's 3,500 people live in dugouts hacked into the sides of the eroded sandstone hills. Coober Pedy wasn't anything at all until 1946, when an Aborigine woman named Tottie Bryant happened upon an eight-mile seam of opal, setting off a stampede of white men. They came from all over, from places like Italy, Greece, and Yugoslavia, furiously humping mining equipment and explosives across the desert. Today there are apparently people from seventy-six nations in Coober Pedy, lustily digging holes in the baked earth, gnawing out the brilliant stone that the ancient Greeks called *opallios*, "to see a change."

Because the guidebook tells us to, we stop in at Crocodile Harry's lair, "an interesting example of a dugout home." Crocodile Harry, it turns out, is in the hospital recovering from a leg injury, but the door is open, and Harry leaves an impression, even in absentia. His lair is a cramped and foul-smelling multiroom cavern with whitewashed walls and a domed ceiling, not unlike a brain cavity. The man's cave reflects the man's mind, showcasing Harry's devotion to erotica, including piles of nudie calendars, nudie posters, and several eight-foot plaster renditions of headless women with watermelon-size boobs, sculpted, it would seem, by Harry himself.

We find ourselves in the bedroom, which features a bed, a small TV, a faded, striped terry robe hanging from a hook, and Harry's "virgin collection," a dizzying collage of more than one thousand women's names, painted on the bony walls and ceiling of his bedroom over many years: SIRPA FROM FINLAND. KISSES FROM DOROTHY. HARRY U STUD—JEAN, BRISBANE. I let out a low whistle; Sugar wrinkles her nose. Farther from the bed, there's a tattered newspaper clipping on the wall. "The best girl will get a prize of a fortnight in my bedroom." Harry, a former croc hunter now in his sixties, has told an Australian paper, "Second prize will be a week in my kitchen." Then this, "They can be pretty near virgins. I'm not that fussy."

The weird gets weirder. We have arranged to meet up at the Italian Club, an aboveground miners' hangout, with Tim Byrnes, the crinkly-eyed redhead we'd met at William Creek. Tim is thirty-one and pale as an Irishman. Originally from Coober Pedy, he's part of a nomadic road crew based outside William Creek. He's now driven his truck four hours here, purportedly to give us an update on road conditions. He'll drive four hours back to report for work at sunrise. We get the distinct feeling we're being courted.

Tim explains that in Coober Pedy the Italians hate the Greeks, the Greeks hate the Italians, and everyone is terrified of the Serbs. The miners tend to be clannish and hostile—a situation compounded by their ready access to explosives. At the local drive-in, this announcement is beamed onto the movie screen nightly: PATRONS: EXPLOSIVES ARE NOT TO BE BROUGHT INTO THIS THEATRE. In the last ten years, the Coober Pedy courthouse, the town hall, and the newspaper offices have been bombed. A Greek restaurant got "bloody totaled," and ditto for the police station. Most recently annihilated were two police cars, which happened to be parked in exactly the spot where our Subaru now rests.

"Shitchyeah! Diesel fuel and fertilizer!" says Tim. "Y'do it to impress yer mates."

A muscly man with a big shrub of a beard then comes by and introduces himself as Karl. He invites us to a party out by the dump, and when we say no, he snatches Sugar's camera from the table and goes swaggering off toward the men's room. "Maybe I'll just put this down my pants and give you Sheilas something royt to look at back in 'Merica!" he shouts. Every miner in the Italian Club—a burly group of about twenty—laughs wolfishly.

I am giving Sugar the eye, and Sugar is giving me the eye back. We try to disengage, but Tim transitions from bombing to kidnapping and murder. A German woman was raped and strangled and tossed down a mine shaft, he says. An Italian woman disappeared even more recently. Sugar is on her feet. I'm scanning the room for Karl and our camera. "They never found the Italian chick, but she probably got tossed, too," Tim continues blithely. "The only way y'get caught is if yer up at the pub, braggin' about whatcha did to 'er."

We wish Tim good luck with all that, recover the camera, and get the hell out.

A FEW SHORT NOTES ON THE SONG OF LIFE

To take my mind off how fast Sugar is driving, I read aloud from the map. We've got the mighty Mount Barry, 269 feet if it's an inch, to the left, and Lake Cadibarrawirracanna, an unseen dried-up pond, some miles to the right. I reel off some of the places named for women—Henrietta Creek, Mount Rebecca, Anna Creek, Lora Creek, Charlotte Waters. Did these Annas and Rebeccas live out here, we wonder, or were they merely figments of cowboy dreams? Their namesakes, these creeks that cover the map like capillaries, are nothing but specters—waterless beds that might fill in a monsoon but otherwise remain as parched and empty as the rest of the land. So much wishful thinking.

Five days now, we've lived this life, on the road breakfast to dinner—eating road food, listening to road music, suffering road headaches. Every bump we hit seems to unloose another courtesy and send it winging out the window. Sugar has stopped excusing her belches; I am stockpiling dirty socks beneath the driver's seat. "We've lost our infrastructure," I say to no one in particular. We are having Tim Tams and baby carrots for breakfast. Sugar eats with one hand and drives with the other. We overtake a slow-moving pickup truck. We never knew life could be this good.

Some hundred million years ago, most of central Australia was underwater, covered by a shallow, lapping sea full of prehistoric wildlife. Driving over bleached, salt-crusted plains, we feel surrounded by Mesozoic ghosts—needle-toothed plesiosaurs and tentacled ammonites, icthyosaurs and nautiloids—baked in and fossilized on all sides. The planet turns toward dusk. We pitch camp behind a roadhouse in Oodnadatta, a predominantly Aborigine town, laid out in a neat grid of weather-worn concrete bungalows. A few children kick a ball around a tarred playground. The adults seem to be shut in their homes, quiet.

Everything I've read about Aborigine culture emphasizes that it's difficult to understand from the outside and nearly impossible to summarize. At its most traditional, Aborigine life involves following the paths of the Ancestors, the creators who sang the land into existence, naming the water holes and wattle trees, the cockatoos, snakes, and honey ants. They roamed the continent, leaving a trail of music behind them. These song lines, it's believed, connect the people to the land, the past to the present. The great aim of one's life is to sing your way to where you belong.

To the west, somewhere between faraway and nearby, a dingo starts to howl. The sky has filled with opals. Sugar and I eye the Wet Ones only to decide against washing. We crawl into our tents and wait for sunlight to crack the other side. All that matters now is the motion.

BABY AMBER AND TWO WHO GOT AWAY

We gas up at the roadhouse in Oodnadatta, which is also the town's one-stop post office, bank, restaurant, campground, general store, and auto shop—all run by a small-framed blonde of about forty named Lynnie Plate. Lynnie and her husband visited Oodnadatta in 1974 as camel-trekking hippies and never left.

"Happens to lots of folks," she tells us cheerfully. "You think your life is headed in one direction and then you end up somewhere else, no worries."

When we mention that today we're turning off the Oodnadatta Track and heading north toward Molly Clark's place, Lynnie loads us up with things from her shelves to deliver on credit to homesteaders along the way. We've got spark plugs for a cowboy named Leon, a bag of mail for another cowboy called Phantom, and mousetraps for two brothers living at Dalhousie Springs. All of it is crammed into what little space is left behind our headrests.

We find Leon on a grassy stretch an hour north of Oodnadatta, riding a Yamaha motorbike on the fringe of a herd of shuffling cattle. His face is so sunburned it looks sooty.

"We're like a couple of soccer moms, dontcha think, Leon?" Sugar joshes.

Leon looks blank. This doesn't really translate. Sugar lays a few explanatory details on him as the cows lumber past and her hair whips high in the wind.

"Aw yeah!" Leon exclaims finally, shaking his head, as if he can't believe he missed it the first time. "Oy getcha now. Mums! Mums watching footy!" He tucks the spark plugs into his shirt, looks at the Subaru, and then revs his bike and shouts a final thought: "It's foin for you Yanks, but I reckon mums here don't care much for footy!"

We play Patsy Cline and tell epic stories. This is the hidden benefit of the road trip: no need to abridge. I give Sugar my romantic history in its entirety and then tell all my friends' love stories too. Sugar psychoanalyzes her old boss and then delivers elaborate plot summaries of a couple of her favorite movies, *From Here to Eternity* and *Tank Girl*. We condemn right-wingers and agree that Madeleine Albright rocks. I point out the fact that Sugar's big high-school crush has grown up to be a nude model. She points out that mine got really fat. Miles pass. Pink cockatoos slip in and out of the sky above. An electric-green lizard skitters across the road. We're living on desert time now, which is to say that time is no longer linear. It crooks and corkscrews toward the monochrome sky. We half expect to meet ourselves—as fifteen-year-olds, as wrinkled old battle-axes—in a blue Subaru, driving the other way.

Eventually we crash-land at Hamilton Station, Phantom's homestead, and hand over the mail just in time for lunch. Lunch is a big plank of fresh-killed beef, pan-fried in our honor by Tim, Phantom's nineteen-year-old ranch hand. Young Tim is beautiful. We love watching him cook. He is blue-eyed, lanky, and shy, under a frayed black hat. He tilts the frying pan and makes the fat sizzle.

Sugar and I are seated at a small Formica-topped table, and Phantom slides us each a cup of tea. He's thirty-three, wiry and unshaven, a hard-drinking bronco rider turned family man, with a dark tan and a battered hat and wayward blond curls.

"You Sheilas been out 'ere long?" he asks. "No? Well, we don't get a lot of you foy-male types, ever." Leaning back in his chair, he hangs a cigarette from his bottom lip. "Rare as rockin'-horse shit, I reckon."

Molly Clark is out here, I mention.

"Molly!" says Phantom's blue-eyed wife, Allison. "Oh, we couldn't tell you a thing 'bout Molly, 'cept she's a pioneer out here. Molly sticks to herself, mostly." She stops bouncing their strapping, flaxen-haired baby, Amber, on her lap for a moment, adding, "The road to her place gets ugly from here. Just watch yerselves."

"Oh, that's OK," Sugar says, with a sweep of her hand. "If we get into trouble, we'll just call for young Tim." The boy's cheeks go crimson.

The kitchen is tidy and spare. A UHF radio high on a shelf reports from other cattle stations while the three of them tell us about ranch life. There is nothing dignified about how I feel just now, eating beef with white bread and ketchup in a little homestead set down on a piece of range that's bigger than Connecticut. I am melting. I am in love with them all. Sugar is mesmerized by Amber.

"She's just like a Nebraska baby," she is telling Allison. This is Sugar's highest praise.

I spend a minute dreaming about how it would feel to get whisked out of my life by a bronco rider named Phantom, to live in a little house on the prairie and have myself a robust farm baby. And then I'm remembering that husbands and babies give me vertigo—it's the same omelette cooked in a more exotic pan. Then I'm not sure. Whatever the case, the road is calling. We've got another day's drive to reach Molly Clark. We help clear the dishes.

Allison walks Sugar and me back to the station wagon. She explains that she was a secretary outside London until she came through the outback on holiday three years ago and bumped into Phantom down at the William Creek Hotel on a Friday night. "I was passin' through, with every intention of going home after a few weeks," she tells us, adjusting Amber on her hip. "Me family can still hardly believe it," she says, a faint smile playing across her face as we climb into the car. "I was just like you."

WHAT BECAME OF MOLLY, PART ONE

For fifteen minutes now we've been sitting at the state border between South Australia and the Northern Territory, docked next to a big orange triangle that says 4WD ONLY! It's 6 A.M.; the land is lit in pink. Sugar's got her nose buried in the Subaru manual, displaying her first interest in written instruction of any kind. It has suddenly become important to understand the difference between the button that says OVERDRIVE and the one that says POWER.

We've come 700 miles without a bit of pavement, no problem, but now we're at a narrow trench of gnashed, moiling mud—the start of a 65-mile trek to Old Andado Station, Molly Clark's homestead. Some folks say Molly is eighty-five; others have her a decade younger. They say she can tune a diesel engine and has sent a 2,000-pound feral camel scampering with a single, ferocious roar. She has lived alone for the last twenty-five years, since her husband died of a heart attack on their property. When travelers hit her doorstep, dirty and exhausted and expecting to be congratulated for whatever hardships they've endured, Molly apparently doesn't bother listening. "Bah, it's good for yeh," is what she says, before turning back to her chores.

Presently, though, we're concerned only with the road. Get stuck in a place like this and it could be days before another soul drifts by. Just east of where we are, those travelers were stranded by rains earlier in the month, requiring airdrops of food and a rescue by Phantom once the downpour stopped. "Bloody pain in the arse" was Phantom's summary.

The sky above us, however, is a cloudless blue. We are into our last 250 miles of driving. We're so dirty it's unbelievable. Sugar's running shoes are so caked with clay it looks like she's got hooves.

There's bulldust in our lungs, bulldust matting our hair and building ridges inside our noses. We're two days past having clean clothes. The back of the station wagon is a rank salad of half-eaten granola bars, dirty T-shirts, mildewy tent apparatus, and unraveling rolls of toilet paper. We feel as battle-worn and capable as an army tank.

At least that's how we felt right up until the moment we sank the Subaru to its belly in mud. What started as intermittent puddles in a field have unexpectedly turned into intermittent fields in a puddle. And suddenly we're on a paddy of grass surrounded by brown water, the rear end of the station wagon submerged, the front end perched tenuously on dry land, aimed like a piece of artillery at the sky. Convinced the car is drowning, Sugar has pulled out all her valuables and piled them on a safe spot of grass. We are scrupulously avoiding conversation and therefore finger-pointing. Instead, we are digging. Sugar is on her knees, using her hands to try to excavate the right front tire from a giant rut. I am rooting rocks out of the mud and tossing them into the watery well beneath the back tires, which are half-swallowed by muck. I am hoping for traction.

Sugar sits back from the tire and tosses the first grenade. "Now would be a good time to have a shovel, *Sara*," she says severely. Back in Adelaide, she handled food stocking; my job was survival miscellany. There are dribbles of sludge stuck in her hair.

Without mentioning whose manicured Nebraskan hands steered us into this mess, I wade into the water, open the tailgate, and start rummaging. We've got every damn tool in the book, but no shovel. I unearth a plastic garden spade and deliver it to Sugar.

"A spade is part of the shovel *family*," I say.

She takes the spade wordlessly and continues her digging. I go back to my rocks. Every ten minutes or so one of us gets into the car and guns the engine, producing bilgewater spray but no motion. Frustrated, Sugar finally wraps her hands around the bumper and, with a mighty groan, actually tries to lift the car out of the mud. Alas, we are going nowhere.

STUCK IN THE MIDDLE OF OUR ROAD

"He didn't get that fat."

"True," Sugar says. "He was already chubby."

We're back to old crushes—and getting no nicer despite the fact that we're moving once again. Miraculously, we were hauled out of our grass paddy by a kindly husband and wife from New South Wales, who are now trailing us in their Land Cruiser as we negotiate the last miles to Old Andado. Mucky plains give way to sand again; we fishtail down a giant dune, and there's Molly's place, a sprawl of shantylike corrugated-iron buildings, winking cheerfully in the sun.

But Molly isn't here. Instead, two young guys come out from inside and give us the once-over. It's not until now that I understand just how startling we are—the Subaru wears a thick carapace of mud; there's a banana-size scrape on one of my arms; Sugar's hair has an electrocuted look to it. After all that digging, our backs are aching fiercely, and we are slumped and frowning. Keeping their distance, the boys explain that Molly broke her hip recently, kicking out a mulga stump. She's recovering in Alice Springs and won't be back for weeks.

"Kicking out a stump, can you imagine?" I say, steering us out of Old Andado and onto our final stretch of desert.

"That's my kind of old lady," Sugar says back. We are friends again.

I spend awhile feeling dejected about missing Molly Clark,

though I can't say exactly why. I had this vision of her, a sweet-faced shotgun-toting octogenarian, caretaker of this wild and lonely outback garden, the pioneer mama we all carry inside. I thought maybe she'd get me excited about my future. But whoever she is, she's simply not here.

Out on the horizon, we can see a lake—a distant Caribbean shimmer in the direction of Alice Springs. The road forks. We head left, only to find that the road splits again. Next we go right and get looped back around, we think, to where we started. Soon we're looking at a series of tire tracks that bifurcate and trifurcate in every direction across the sand. Sugar lets out a giddy laugh. Hand-over-hand on the steering wheel again, I recall a story I heard about a family from Queensland who perished in a situation like this, driving in circles until they ran out of gas, became dehydrated, and died.

Using the lake as a landmark, I spin us back toward the water and hit the gas. The station wagon bucks into gear and launches. What we don't understand yet is that we're hurtling toward an apparition, sunlight glancing off acres of dried earth. Maybe there's water out there somewhere, but perhaps it's only the promise of water, the memory of water. The point is, the road has vanished behind us, and we're not thinking about how to find it again. Point is, we are suspended in this weird nothingness, the tinsel shine of some illusory lake trembling and darting like a mercury blob ahead of us, far away and never getting closer.

WHAT BECAME OF MOLLY, PART TWO

It's about showers and phones now. The sun sets, the illusions dissolve, and the road returns beneath the wheels of the Subaru. We hit pavement just outside Alice Springs and let up a hoot. We pass

Kmart and KFC and shops full of Aborigine tchotchkes. Sweet heaven, we're going to bathe! We find a hotel, swank by outback standards, with a pool and a pen of dazed-looking kangaroos for petting.

Sugar gets her cricket player on the phone and I dance into a steaming bath. Sunk in wondrous clear water, I do a little archeology, recovering my body from the layers of caked-on earth. Everything we do has a certain last-night deliciousness to it. We eat fried barramundi and sing "Waltzing Matilda" with a crowd of paved-road tourists at the local steakhouse. We wash it all down with cold stubbies. When sleep comes, it is deep and full, the two of us knocked sideways and unconscious by the full weight of our fatigue.

In the morning, I drive a combed and lipsticked Sugar to the airport.

"Bye, lovely," she says, bear-hugging. Then there's that schnort again.

With a few hours before my own flight out, I try one last time to find Molly Clark. There's a listing for her in the Alice Springs phone book. Her voice is a ratchety squall. I explain that I just drove 1,300 miles through the outback on the chance that I might get to see her.

She says, not unwisely, "Well, that's bloody pathetic, isn't it?"

She'll give me fifteen minutes and a cup of tea.

"Is there a certain time that's more convenient?"

"I don't have a flaming clue what's convenient!" Molly Clark roars.

OK, then.

I'm at her doorstep now, working up the nerve to knock. It's a tiny bungalow on a quiet side street. I try to think of what it is I want to ask Molly, or say to her, but it all seems suddenly childish. I consider bolting. Bolting sounds like a good idea, a grown-up one. But through the screen door comes a voice: "You that 'Merican girl called me on the phone?"

She's there, deep in the green shadows of her kitchen, bent over the sink, peeling potatoes. I squint through the screen. "It's me," I say. Molly does not turn to look. Sun filters through a pair of chintz curtains, lighting the storm of white hair on her head, the thick glass of her spectacles. She skins another potato and drops it emphatically into a pot of water. There's a pile of carrots on the counter nearby, and I can see through the shadows that Molly uses a walker to get around. I realize then that she could be anybody, there in her kitchen, an old lady from the outback or my own suburban grandmother from Philly. Just another tough old bird. I pass an awkward minute on Molly Clark's threshold. Until, with the tiniest swell of a smile, she invites me inside.

HOOK, LINE, AND PINKER: WETTING A LINE IN CUBA

••

Holly Morris

I'm lodged in the corner of the terminal folded up like an accordion, head propped on a backpack, studying my Spanish phrase book—although I'm told cramming will do little good because even native Spanish speakers have trouble with the Cuban accent. I'm on the As, and it occurs to me that the word for "adventure," *aventura,* has a certain girl tenor. The concept has certainly played out that way for me.

As a child chasing trout in the soggy Northwest with my grandmother, I learned about fishing and companionship. She taught me how to thread worms on hooks, *and* how to view the world with political precision. Balancing *The New York Times* on her knees, she'd soak up the latest minutiae of the Watergate scandal while awaiting her prey.

"Take that, Tricky Dick!" she'd suddenly bellow, rocking boats a mile away as she reeled in her hapless catch.

During Illinois teendom I led my girlfriends on an annual fishing trip to Wisconsin where we revered nameless gray ponds and their sluggish bass as if they were divinity-kissed Rocky Mountain lakes filled with wily trout. Of course, Wisconsin's drinking age, eighteen, influenced our choice of location, but we did manage to wet lines and our whistles. Because our sensibilities were minted in the crucible of Watergate and divorce, we were cynical about the pillars of family and state. We were much more comfortable lionizing one another. We left behind our broken homes, and the clatter receded to a dull hum as we created our own rituals. Adventure became a vehicle for independence and escape, and that ever undervalued currency of liberation: fun. Friendship trumped all else. Without knowing it, we were tilling some pretty serious Zen soil.

Fifteen years later, folded up in Seattle's Sea Tac airport on a drizzly predawn morning, negatively wired on fatigue and stress, it occurs to me that ambition has turned my Zen soil to mud. The bolt of clarity that struck in a Sumatran jungle and inspired a new career phase—to ditch desk life and travel the world creating a television series called *Adventure Divas*—has long since faded. On this eve of landing in Cuba, with miles of red tape fluttering in my wake, I think that having fun has never been this hard before, and I wonder: can adventure be institutionalized? Shifting anxiously in the departure lounge, I tick through my bring-along list: passport (check), cash (check), attitude adjustment (I'm working on it). Ordinarily the sum total of essentials for any adventure ends here, but this time the list has lengthened considerably to include two cinematographers, a load of 16 mm film, a producer, and a sound person. We're 200 pounds overweight, but a healthy gratuity blinds the check-in man to our infraction, and we are on our way.

As we jog down the gangway my stomach plummets. Oh my

God. I've forgotten my fly rod. I've kept a rod in my trunk since I was sixteen, toted it across countless state lines, even continents. To what lapse of character, I ask myself, do I owe a blunder as serious as leaving behind my rod?

Wailing over my stupidity, I turn to cinematographer Cheryl Dunn, the crew member I expect to be most simpatico.

"Whatever," she responds, with full-on New Yorker sympathy.

After two connecting flights we finally board the Yak 42 Soviet plane bound for the forbidden isle. The Yak is a chamber of chaos: broken seats, frayed seatbelts. Smoke billows around our legs on takeoff.

I forget about the fly rod.

A NEW BRAND OF ICON

We wander and immerse ourselves in Havana's decayed opulence. I note that there are lots of arches, but none of them are golden. "Just think," I say to Cheryl, "ninety miles from the coast of Florida, no neon, no advertising, no Bill Gates wondering 'Where Do We Want To Go Today.'"

Cuba does, however, rival the United States in the icon worshiping department. The dashing Argentine revolutionary Che Guevara gazes intently over public squares and is lionized on every peso. Intelligent, sensitive, literary he was—or so the legend goes. In an easier time, Che definitely would have been a fly fisher. Cheryl dubs him *El Guapo Hombre* (handsome man) and tells me how she wants to hitch across South America with his book *The Motorcycle Diaries* as her only companion. Ironically, the living Fidel Castro's image is not prominently displayed, yet "El Lider" is omnipresent, like oxygen: all around and influencing everything.

Cheryl and I are laboriously translating a Marxist slogan, HASTA LA VICTORIA SIEMPRE, which is splashed across the side of a building, when a young man walks up.

"*De donde eres*? Canada? England?" he says.

"Los Estados Unidos," Cheryl responds cautiously. He is surprised, but friendly. "The bar where Hemingway drank mojitos every afternoon is right around the corner." Hemingway. Thus, the trifecta of Cuba's male cultural icons is complete. I zealously explain that we're more interested in finding our own brand of icon: divas. "We want to interview women who are inspired and accomplished, who don't wait for their ships to come in but row out and meet them—you know, *divas*." The man backs away slowly, smiling kindly, and walks off.

COMRADE DUNN

One evening, over our usual dinner of chicken, beans, and rice, it occurs to me that there is water water everywhere but I've yet to see fish on a menu. Our sound person, Pam, who is a walking encyclopedia, tells me, "When the Soviets evaporated and famine became a real threat here, Fidel tried to offset the cultural bias against fish eating by handing out fish recipes on slips of paper wherever he went. Didn't work." The wheels start turning: If Cubans don't eat much fish, and don't sport-fish, then Cuba's fish have been growing fat for the past three decades! No *gringas* like me, or Hemingway wannabes, overfishing the waters. This is an interesting and providential side effect of Cuba's political isolation.

Cheryl, a lanky, dark, and insatiably curious fashion photographer cum cinematographer from New York, queries me about my fishing fascination. "What exactly is the attraction?" she says with friendly sarcasm. "The five A.M. call time? The icy waters? The slime?"

At the risk of sounding like a hackneyed spiritual dilettante, I explain rhythm and meter, and angling's strangely satisfying intellectual netherland. Boldly I wax poetic about the scrumptious pandemonium of the take, how worldly troubles slough away; the honor of tangoing with a primeval creature from another world.

She looks at me blankly. "I respect your passion," she says, "but I don't get it." In most matters we are in sync, but our friendship is definitely still in the circling, sniffing stage.

Cheryl and I are the youngest members of our small band of filmmakers. Born in the mid-sixties, she and I grew up on lessons lean on Cuban history, so we have a hazy, limited vision of this pinko outpost. Throughout most of our lives the U.S. media coverage of Cuba has offered little more than a bunch of de-contextualized buzzwords: Bay of Pigs, Cuban Missile Crisis, Mariel boat lift, Fatigues versus Suit, . . . and, of course, cigars and salsa.

Cheryl and I soon establish a pattern of occasional escape from the rest of our posse. On these happy *aventuras* we weave in and out of Havana's potholed byways admiring the funky prerevolutionary De Sotos and Edsels that chug through the city. Of our crew, Cheryl best lives the notion that work and play can be one and the same, and this spirit shows in her film. I watch her as she swings her Bolex like a maestro, celluloid soaking up the muted colors and gritty textures of Havana's weathered buildings. She develops instant rapport with her subjects and ends up dancing with them as often as filming them. Cheryl shoots from the hip, literally, and I'm beginning to understand why *Vogue* magazine voted her New York's most stylish fashion photographer a few years back (despite the fact that she's a thrifter who won't wear anything that costs more than $5). Cheryl's style comes from within.

When it's time to head out of Havana we discover the state-run rail system, as jam-packed as it is unscheduled. Cubans needing rides stand about on corners to flag down cars. In the *campo*, however, cars are rare, so for a peso or two, people pack into the beds of old Russkie trucks that belch smoke. We enter the competition by doing what Norte Americanos do in a foreign country with an economy that is shot to hell: we unlace our boots, pull out our carefully hidden and not too fragrant wad of twenties, and flash some Yankee greenbacks. Edsel it is.

The crew settles into a rhythm. We stumble through the tiring yet invigorating cultural dance that comes with hard travel. Some days we are broken down by adversity; then we rebuild into something stronger. Cuba's many graces come alive as we meet a politically charged young rap trio, a poet who defies the forces that would squash her free expression, a Black Panther in exile, and a Santeria Priestess.

Long, sweaty days end with whispered quotes to Cheryl from my *Moon Handbook:* "Cuba is a sleeper with fresh water lakes and lagoons that almost *boil* with tarpon, bonefish, snook, and bass."

"What," Cheryl asks, pausing from writing in her journal, "is a snook?"

BUENA PESCADORA!

Weary after weeks of filming I pull rank and, pleading crew respite, steer our road trip off course to Lake ZaZa.

Cheryl tosses me a knowing look.

The lodge we find has a Khrushchev-does-the-Caribbean kind of flair. Within an hour Cheryl has struck up a friendship and is behind the bar learning how to make mojitos (rum, sugar, *yerba buena*, lime, and more rum). I surreptitiously lobby her. "Listen to this," I say, "'Americans fishing home waters apparently catch, on average, only one bass every two days of fishing. During those same two days a bass fisherman at Lake ZaZa might expect to catch one hundred bass of incredible quality. *There's a good chance that a world record bass exists in Cuba.*'"

"Okay," she agrees with a smile, "I'll go fishing—but I'm just going to watch." Wired like a kid at Christmas, I wake up at 4:30 the following morning. "Cheryl," I whisper, and shake her, "the eagle has landed." We tiptoe by our sleeping colleagues. I put on my best Hemingway swagger and calling up five weeks of intensive Spanish—and on a tip from last night's bartender—I go in search of a man named Cheo.

Cheo is old, weather-worn, and his gait conveys a blend of resignation and dignity. The romantic in me calls up the image of Hemingway's Santiago in *The Old Man and the Sea* even though it turns out Cheo has a boat with a motor (not a skiff with a sail) and a rod (not a long line), and, most notably, he is fishing for a living (not living for a fish). But, like Santiago, Cheo speaks not a word of English.

As dawn breaks we motor out for the morning bite. Pink skies. Calm waters. Mimed promises of *bigguns*. Though I knew my fly-fishing brethren would abhor what was to be my near blood-bait fall from grace, I still am not prepared for the massive lure that will take the place of my usual tiny nymph. Cheo dangles an eight-inch-long obscenely pink and very barbed rubber worm in front of our faces. Cheryl blanches.

The effete fly fisher in me is horrified—but my inner angler, bred on Midwestern bass and candy-striped Mepps, screams out in carnal joy: These Fish Must Be Enormous!

I start casting.

Cheryl finesses her cameras like a musician before the big performance, then stops, as if she's received a signal from some cosmic maestro.

The sun breaches the horizon and the water gently laps against the boat. Time is metered by the reel's muted clicks. We do not comment, or joke, or even look at one another. And it is in this companionable quiet that the cards of friendship definitively shuffle into place. It is one thing to know you can work together, and entirely another to know you can be silent together.

Strangely, I feel as if the whole trip—the hitchhiking, the relentless heat, the camaraderie, the interviews—has led up to this moment. The road drill has prepared me. Cheryl reminded me that work and play *can* be one and the same, and this time-worn angling ritual has brought me back to myself. The moment hangs in the intangible equity of friendship.

Suddenly, a hit sends my forearm plunging toward the floorboards, and the tenuous moment collapses in on itself. A tank of a fish, but a fighter nonetheless, the *pescado* I hook has me waltzing around the tiny boat, Cheo following my lead, net in hand. As the battle rages, Cheo manages to light a cigar, and a boatful of loud Italians moves into our honey hole. Cheryl bobs and weaves, filming and giggling. "Yeee haaaw," she yells from behind her camera. Cheo seems nonplussed, but my endorphins fire with each and every centimeter of line the fish takes. *Chica* against fish. A beating sun. The mighty swordfish (well—I mean bass). A duel of passion and nobility, and increasingly, ego. And then, to put it in spare Hemingwayesque prose . . . I win.

I haul in the glistening large-mouthed bass and am breathless at its size. The fish tops twelve pounds, dwarfing the measly bass of my youth. *"Buena pescadora!"* Cheo yells out from one corner of the boat; and Cheryl keeps repeating with Manhattan awe, "Oh my God. Oh my God."

On the way back to the lodge, just as the last traces of morning light's magic veil burn off, Cheryl says, "But . . . it's not about the fish."

I smile and respond, "Whatever."

TWO ROADS HOME

••

BK Loren

UNPAVED

The desert sky, round and blue as it is on summer days, was still round and blue when my school day was over. I closed my locker door and walked the solitary dirt road to my home on the mesa. From there I gathered my kayak, spray skirt, paddle, and helmet, and hiked down into the gorge of the Rio Grande.

As rivers age, their banks widen like a woman's hips; their waters meander a slower, more forgiving course. In river time, the northern New Mexico stretch of the Rio Grande is young. At only a few hundred million years of age, it's an adolescent at best. It runs white and fast, class four most of the way—except for Sunset Rapids. Two winters ago a storm surged through a side canyon and dumped boulders and tree trunks into the Sunset section, turning it from class four to class five overnight. To a kayaker, risking a "wet exit" (bailing out of your boat) in class five waters means risking, maybe, your life.

I liked that. For the same reasons I liked climbing El Cap and mountain biking downhill without pulling the brakes. Death wish? Not a chance. I loved the precision these sports demanded; I saw every river run, mountain-biking trip, and climbing route as an expression of my love for this delicious life. I wanted to taste it all. The salty, bitter, unwanted edges of it. I wanted to feel my muscles stretch my skin taut, to fix my mind into resolute focus. I paddled the Rio Grande at dusk, sometimes making it to Sunset Rapids at twilight when the waning light erased the shadows that defined the contours of the river, and picking a line was like navigating through a circus mirror. The clouds on the horizon reflected red in the river, and I paddled through the wound of twilight.

I had tried more conventional sports—things that involved balls. But at some point I always lost my concentration and became absurdly aware of myself running around on a wooden floor, investing meaning and value and every bit of energy I had into manipulating the course of an inflated ball. I was supposed to run like hell to smash the racquetball against the front wall, kick the soccer ball into the net, send the baseball sailing above the outfield. But the ball meant nothing to me. The pursuit of it did not involve risking my life. The rules were arbitrary.

PAVED

In Northlake, the closed-in Chicago suburb where I lived, there was no clock tower, no cathedral music on the hour, no chimes. Instead, low jets from O'Hare flew over our rooftops every fifteen minutes, ticking away time in a deafening roar. The territory of Northlake consisted of industrial buildings, fast-food joints that sold kolacky, kielbasa, eggrolls, and pizza—on the same menu—and a clutch of houses filled with families named Ensilacco, Zobiach, Cozeiule, Wasczalowski, Chang, and Čech—all of us less than two generations away from our homelands, and several generations away from the American dream.

People didn't live in Northlake; they remained. Not quite American enough to know we could relocate whenever we wanted, we stayed. When property values dropped, we stayed; when taxes went up, we stayed. When our voices were drowned out by that steady stream of low-flying jets, we talked louder, and we stayed.

There was a creek nearby my house in Northlake. It ran either sudsy, like dishwater, or smelly, like sulfur; those were your two choices. That was my introduction to nature. I didn't like it.

But I loved Northlake. It was my home. I had friends, and my friends and I had something very important in common: hoops. From the time I was five, I met Gail, Burma, Dimitra, and Lui on any paved surface—the street, an industrial driveway, a parking lot—and we played. Net or no net, we played, because basketball is not just about getting the ball into the hoop. It's about moving down the court, cutting left or right, crossover dribbling, defense and offense and more defense. With a little imagination, the goal becomes secondary.

But between sixth grade and seventh grade, things changed. Not for me, but for the other girls. They lost interest in hoops and grew fond of makeup and boys. They met under the bridge and smoked cigarettes, pleased with the imprint their red lipstick made on the cork-colored filter, the way their long fingers cradled the white paper, the trail of smoke drifting from their full lips. I crossed the same bridge on my way home from school. I waved to Gail, my best friend, or rather, my former best friend, who rolled her eyes and swore that she had never really liked me anyway. I shrugged, continued home, the sound of my tennies slapping the bridge, my basketball dribble resounding like embarrassment in my ex–best friend's ears.

When I came to a wall or any sort of barricade, I imagined a hoop there. I practiced my layup, my jump shot, my follow-through, just as I had done for the past eight years. But the same boys from across town who used to pick me first when we were choosing teams whispered and laughed as they passed by me now. I continued shooting, hoop or no hoop, teammates or none.

At home, I lay on my bed, tossing the ball at a single spot on the ceiling, my wrist curved and flexible, guiding the ball through the final second of contact, the perfect release. One hundred and one, one hundred and two, one hundred and three. If I missed, I started over. My goal was five hundred hits, dead center, perfect follow-through, no room for error.

The whole city was paved. Except, of course, for my driveway, which was gravel. We were too poor to afford paving, or to afford a classy store-bought orange hoop, so my father and Billy, the neighborhood nerd (a gentle boy who was also an outcast by the time sixth grade rolled around), helped me rig a basketball hoop using an old bicycle rim. We mounted it on plywood and hung it above the gravel drive. "The uneven surface will help your ball control," my dad said. He was right. By the time I was twelve I was already dreaming of a college scholarship.

I played at night in "dangerous" parts of the city. I played in winter, the ball splashing into slush, my high-tops slipping off ice. I knew every court within a twenty-mile range, knew when I could pick up a game there, when I could practice alone, when I could play one-on-one.

I made a new set of friends. Our connection was not about sharing secrets or gossiping about others. Actually, we didn't talk much about anything. Everything was said in the grace of movement, the way we, as a team, sometimes breathed as a single organism, the way whoever had the ball dished it to whoever was playing "out of her head" that night, the way we worked, the way we moved, together.

Some people would say it wasn't a life or death thing, but for me, it was. I could take losing my position as the most popular girl on my block. I could handle hours of English class, stacks of homework, endless requests to wear a dress and act like a lady, as long as I knew that at the end of the day I could play ball. When I danced out of my English honors class early one day, my teacher followed me with threats. "You'll never get into college that way, little missy." But she was raised upper class, and I was on my way to play hoops. Without a scholarship, I'd never see a university; I'd never have the life she took for granted.

SEMI-PAVED

Lisa and I met at a gym, and we were both a little shell-shocked, because after our first two months in California the Loma Prieta earthquake hit. It ripped my house in two and sent my personal belongings scuttling down a hillside into a gully. That earthquake is the only reason I signed up at a gym—something about the land slipping out from underneath my feet made me crave the illusion of stability that being indoors offers. But I had yet to learn to move with grace in such a crowded environment, and somewhere between the pedalers on immobile bikes and the sweaty bodies draped over the stair-climbing machines, I tripped over Lisa's foot.

"Sorry," I said.

"No problem. Do you play sports?" she said.

"What?"

"Do you play sports? You know, like hoops or anything?"

"I run rivers," I said. I could see by the look on her face that she was trying to picture me on ice skates, running on the surface of a river—or maybe I wore skis, or the latest brand of river-running shoes. Whatever the image, I was speaking a foreign language to her ears. But I was new to the area, and her warm if awkward hello let me know she was reaching out.

"I like racquetball," I said.

Weeks later we met on the racquetball court, and without breaking a sweat she scored some 64 points in a matter of twenty minutes while I, panting like a beagle, scored 10. The only real competition was between my humiliation and her boredom.

"How about mountain biking?" I said when our match (or lack thereof) was over.

"I don't have a bike," she said.

"We could play racquetball again."

"I can borrow a bike," she said

The following weekend we pedaled to our meeting place on the coast of northern California where the mountains are molehills but the trees gain elevations unimaginable. Redwoods spired and disappeared into the cool October fog, and thousands of monarch butterflies fluttered around us, their amber, gold, red, and black wings like autumn leaves that would never die but would drift forever upward. The mountain biking was secondary. I had this fledgling friendship, this day, this season. I pulled my front tire over a small ledge then cruised down a tiny hill. The mist turned to rain on my face. At the bottom of the hill, I turned to Lisa to share my elation. But I was alone. "Lisa?" I looked around. "Lisa?" I looked up. She had just finished lifting her mountain bike over the tiny lip of concrete and was now standing stiff as a stone monument on top of the hill. "C'mon," I called. No response. I rode back to the top. "What's up?"

"Nothing."

"Let's go."

"No."

"No?"

"I'm not riding this down that hill."

"It's not a hill, really. It's a mound."

"With rocks in it. Huge rocks." The rocks were slightly larger than my fist.

Fifteen minutes later, we were at the bottom, and my ears hurt from the constant screech of her brakes as she squeezed them tightly and inched her way down the hill. Even the butterflies scattered from the sound.

THE BRIDGE

I am, by nature, a loner, and I need little more than a tarp over my head, a pen, and some paper. I've always believed that the solitary Woman-in-Nature pose I've assumed was a position of courage. But over the past decade my relationship with Lisa has become the single most important relationship of my life, and through it I have learned. I've learned that every time Lisa stepped onto the court with a group of other women, she was challenging every social more about how women should behave: they should ice-skate or play tennis, not compete in soccer or hoops; they should wear skirts as they play; they should not team up, because women do not know how to work together as a team. They are competitive *against* one another, not together toward a common goal. They are solitary creatures, at the same time docile and dangerous; they are not to be trusted, like cats. In the same year that Chris Evert took home millions of dollars from the tennis court, Lisa graduated from college and took a desk job because at that time the New York Liberty was just a dream in some radical's back pocket. Through Lisa I've learned how teams are dangerous, and going solo can sometimes be a safer course. I've also learned about a new kind of wilderness.

Before her, I rarely went outdoors without climbing a five-ten or kayaking a class four. The perfection demanded, the concentration required, the adrenaline spent, these things kept me alive and pushed me to new endeavors. I wanted to see everything, do everything; I wanted to dip my body in every sensation and come out on the other side—calm, transformed, a better person. Mick Jagger once said his greatest fear was boredom. The same sentiment resonated in my mind like the lyrics to a pop song, or a mantra that had gone unscrutinized. And while I remained vigorously attached to the wilds, Lisa remained attached to hoops and Chicago. "You can take the girl out of Chicago, but you can't take Chicago out of the girl," she'd remind me.

"Yeah, yeah," I'd say. "Chicago's a city."

But a city, of course, is a place, and while I was attached to my next outdoor rush and all the high-tech equipment it took for me to get that rush, Lisa was attached to a home. People remain in Northlake, even when they live elsewhere; they order kolacky and pizza from Chicago to Colorado via overnight Federal Express; they hear jet noise as a kind of music that whisks them away to childhood nostalgia and their days in the hood. With Lisa, I learned to stay. Each day I settled deeper into something more permanent, more wild, and more like a home within myself.

Likewise, Lisa changed, though I can't remember when or why. The first time I asked if she'd like to join me on a hike, she said, "No, I need to get some exercise today." Now I sometimes wake on weekend mornings to find our two dogs sitting in the car along with our daypacks, loaded and ready to go. She gathers my hiking shorts and boots and helps me, in my blissful Sunday morning lethargy, dress and get out the door so we can be the first ones on the trail. On occasion she skips a televised Bulls game in favor of snowshoeing or cross-country skiing. At the end of a day outdoors, her muscles are sore, and she is tired. She admits, not even reluctantly, that, yes, walking uphill is a workout, and scoring more points than the other team pales in comparison to many things—among them, the rare peregrines that circled above the canyon we hiked weekly this summer; the day in New Mexico when the wind gusted the rim of the Rio Grande gorge and the ravens positioned themselves on treetops, opened their wings, and were lifted effortlessly into the blue, where they tucked their wings in and tumbled, weightlessly, through the sky. We watched them over and over again, for hours. We were silent, taken away. She admits that hitting the game-winning shot is exhilarating, but not as exhilarating as the simple sight of the black bear we saw on the mountainside, nuzzling the ground for bugs. When her life doesn't make sense to me, when I can't fathom not craving nature and all the drama and serenity it offers, she says, "You can't choose what is not offered to you." Then I search for someone to thank—fate, my parents, God?—for blessing me with what I have all too often taken for granted: this wilderness in my heart, these ever shrinking open spaces, these choices.

PATHS IN AN OPEN SPACE

I learned to enjoy traditional, non-cutting-edge sports: hot, sweaty basketball games inside a gym on a snowy January evening; baseball and soda pop on a sweltering summer evening; a simple hike in the woods in spring. This was not nostalgia; I was not looking backward and selecting only the sweet-smelling roses from the stinky compost of necessary rot. I was looking ahead. I didn't need to be on edge in order for my mind to click into focus anymore.

The minute I allowed my quick world to blur, it refocused on its own: minuscule flowers mapped my hikes like nighttime constellations; they filled me with awe. The mountains filled me with awe. A deer turd filled me with awe.

It was like this: before enlightenment, chopping wood; after enlightenment, chopping wood. I'm not laying any claim to enlightenment. I'm just saying that what takes place between the before and the after is what makes everything possible now.

Now is when I met Lisa.

Our house is on open space: two hundred acres and three ponds that the state promises will remain undeveloped "in perpetuity." Every day for the past half-decade Lisa and I have walked this land together. The place is a necessary paradise for our dogs, Bo and Mo, and it has become, for us, something numinous. It was through this small patch of land that Lisa discovered life beyond the basketball courts of Chicago and I discovered the thrill of the routine rituals of daily life. We walk slowly, nothing for Lisa to compete with, no high risk to keep me on edge.

In the field with Lisa, Bo, and Mo, the awareness I loved when climbing or kayaking kicks in without prompting. I hear the low, hollow sound whistling beneath the surface of frozen ponds; I smell the damp, woody scent of the winter air that lingers into early spring. Not driven to constantly explore new territories, I have finally remained in one place long enough to watch a pair of great blue herons teach their gawky, adolescent offspring how to hunt. I watch season after season. By fall, that same gawky, adolescent offspring fledges into a form of beauty, grace, and perfection that I can never fully comprehend.

In midwinter we walk beneath the knotted branches of bare trees where ferruginous hawks roost, their dark feathers puffed up against the cold. We see signs of foxes, their straight, narrow tracks, scraps of their reddish-gray fur, occasionally the black tips of their tails that disappear into the distance before we can name them. We watch bald eagles fly low over the ponds, their yellow beaks and dark silhouettes like apparitions behind the falling snow.

I watch Bo run with Lisa, and I memorize the way Bo galumphs, buries her nose in the snow, stops, buries it deeper, then resurfaces with a face full of white. I memorize Lisa's walk, the way she wears the hood of her faded college letter jacket over her head, the way she crouches on all fours and laughs as Bo barrels through the snow at her, both Bo and Lisa tumbling down the powdered hillside. These days are holy if anything ever was. This is my family. Bo, Mo, Lisa, the field, the ponds, the wildlife, my family.

A DETOUR TOWARD UNDERSTANDING

I'm not sure we knew what we were looking for, but I know we found it when we came to this land. Though Lisa sometimes pines away for the chance to play basketball under the halo of a July street lamp on Chicago blacktop, she spends her off-work hours striving diligently to protect and preserve the wildlife of this land and other areas in Colorado. Although the changes I went through are, of course, easy for me to comprehend, her transformation sometimes puzzles me. It seems to me the wilderness has always been here, and with any luck it will always be here. It's the simplest thing in the world to do—to step outside with nothing more than a backpack and a few snacks to hold you over. It's a matter of will, available to anyone who opens her back door. If Lisa loves the wilderness now, why didn't she love it then?

The way I came to understand it is this:

I work as a naturalist for state parks on occasion. A few weeks ago a community service worker was assigned to our area to do litter pickup and maintenance. The kid drove the narrow dirt road to the visitors center on a snowy winter day, and when he arrived he was visibly shaken.

"That road's scary," he said. "We don't get that kind of thing back home."

I had to crank my head completely upward to meet his eyes; he was seven feet tall, well muscled, in school on a basketball scholarship. "Chicago winters are really messy," I said.

"Messy, yeah. But they're flat and paved," he said.

He was driving a four-wheel-drive SUV. I smiled, asked him if he had any gloves, and when he said no I gave him a pair. I showed him his assigned tasks then left him for the day.

A few hours later he sprinted into the visitors center. "I saw a mountain lion," he said.

"Yeah?" I said, knowing he hadn't. It was midday and he had been working about fifty feet in front of the visitors center. "Let's go see."

On the way, he described the incident to me. "I saw it coming down the mountain, and I thought it was a regular house cat."

"Was it the size of a house cat?" I asked.

"No. My eyes just couldn't figure out how to see it. I'm telling you, this cat was about a hundred pounds."

His description started to sound like a mountain lion. Neither the ranger, the park manager, nor I had ever seen a mountain lion, though we'd longed to. One season we saw tracks across the frozen stream every morning. They were mountain lion tracks all right—round, lobed at the base, no claws. But we'd never spotted the lion.

The community service worker and I walked on. He took me to the spot where, minutes earlier, he'd seen a cat. I looked down, saw the sign: three lobes, no claws, deep imprint. I was surprised. I was envious.

When I told him he'd seen a lion, he went weak in the knees. I thought he might not return to finish work the following day. But he returned every day for a week. On Friday, he arrived early.

"This is your last day of community service," I said. "Why don't you take off so you can make your basketball practice."

"No," he said. "I like it here."

"You got used to driving that road?"

"Nah, but I will. I've never spent any time outdoors before," he said. "I have a feeling you'll be seeing me around here a lot."

He left late that evening, well past the time he owed the community. I watched his SUV snake down the canyon road, mud slushing up on either side of it, the back tires slipping toward the edge of the canyon in the slick mud.

I told Lisa the story about the community service worker, the lion, and the transformation that seemed to occur in him just from being outdoors for a week. She identified with the young man.

"It's sneaky manipulation," she said, "the way cities offer so much, and at the same time, they turn what's most essential to your spirit into a foreign land."

NEW TERRITORY

This summer, Lisa and I will watch the herons again, and next winter, the foxes.

In our ten years together, I've never been able to convince Lisa that sleeping outdoors is safe, but that matters little to me. Perhaps, in time, we will sleep outdoors together and it will feel safe for both of us. We'll lie on the banks of a river with the coolness of the earth seeping through our sleeping bags. The river will sound like the only music we've ever heard. It will be like this: before enlightenment, chopping wood; after enlightenment, chopping wood. And we'll be where we've always been together: we'll be home.

BREAKING THE ICE

••

Pam Houston

It's March 21, 1998, a day known to scientists and pagan worshipers as the vernal equinox, the day the Sun rises and sets at zero degrees latitude, along the Earth's equator, or more precisely, the day the Earth spins on its axis perfectly perpendicular to the Sun. Today, the Sun is above the flat horizon for exactly twelve hours; tomorrow, it will be up there just a little bit longer.

As a person who finds her faith in the consistency in the patterns of the universe, and as an acute sufferer of seasonal affective disorder, this is a big day for me. Maybe the biggest. On December 21 I feel a measure of relief, because even though I have most of the winter in front of me, I know that with each passing day, unbearably short as it is, it will be light for a little bit longer. On September 21 I feel nothing but flat-out panic that we are about to enter the long slide into darkness that feels like nothing short of a survival test each year. People think June 21 should be a seasonal-affected person's happiest day, but it's really joy mixed with trepidation. It may be the beginning of summer, but each day will get a little shorter from there on in. March 21 is the only truly joyful day . . . twelve hours of daylight and nothing but clear sailing ahead.

In the winter I rise at first light each morning, spend as many hours outside as the weather allows, taking advantage of every moment of light the stingy heavens offer. But soon there will be so much daylight I won't know what to do with it. I might sleep in every so often. I might even take a nap in the middle of the afternoon.

My friend Marilyn is visiting from Boston—a place with winters far darker than here—and we are celebrating the equinox together. What this has involved so far is walking each day the half a mile to the creek that borders my property, hanging over the edge of the bridge, and throwing rocks at the ice until holes start to form. The weather here has been changeable, which means brilliant sunshine mixed with snow squalls so thick and sudden that you can't see your hand in front of your face.

What started out as the casual tossing of a few rocks over the edge has turned, over the course of the last five days, into something far more serious. Now we are hauling boulders the size of microwave ovens up onto the bridge. We are taking turns—one of us bracing herself against the bank and holding on to the other's arm while the other ventures out onto the ice and stamps its edges for all she is worth.

We have gone through several pairs of pants and shoes each, and with all the rocks we have moved this week we feel we may have seriously put into jeopardy the structural security of the bridge. None of these things seems important. We are on a mission. We are two women with seasonal affective disorder doing what we can to make spring come.

••

If anyone had told me five years ago, when my best girlfriend Sally died from breast cancer, that it would take me five years to let another woman this far into my life, I would have said that person was insane. I knew Sally's death had rocked me hard, coming as it did only eight months after the sudden death of my mother and a few months before the end of my marriage.

When my mother died, my husband Mike said, "You don't really have to go into therapy about this because you have me to talk to." When Sally died he said, "Well, you knew she was going to die for so long that you've done all your grieving. You should be fine from now on." Three years later I found out that the real reason he was so down on therapy was that he had slept with the therapist I eventually started seeing—in those days, one of the few in town. But at the time I took his advice and avoided everything, a list that eventually included him and any potential women friends that might come my way.

I made friends, in those years, with men—they didn't have breasts and seemed therefore immune to cancer. I had mammograms I didn't need, spent way too much money on health insurance, and waited for the inevitable diagnosis that would do me in. My mother had always said about my father, "He's so mean, he'll outlive both of us," and so far he's outlived her by six years. With my father well into his eighties now, I believed that my mother's prophecy sealed the fate I had already imagined. It took me years to understand that not absolutely everything my mother said would come true.

I've never been very good at what my mother used to call the "negative emotions": sadness, anger, frustration, fear. In the house where I grew up, my mother and I weren't allowed to have these feelings. My father made up for our deficiency in the "negative emotions" by having his own all the time.

In the last several years, it seems, I've grown into frustration, had a sortie or two into anger, I've been working really hard to get fear into my repertoire, but sadness (a thing much different than depression) still eludes me.

If I had gone to therapy when Sally died, sadness might have been the first thing I worked on. Now five years later it's the last holdout, the voice in my head, my mother's or mine, still saying, we must never admit to how sad we are; if we do we will die from grief.

I suppose it is possible that if as a child I had let myself feel sad about the things that were happening to and around me, I might have laid down and died from it. But I'm thirty-six now, a woman with my own life, and never is too long not to have the experience of being sad. It's not coming easy to me, and I don't know which I fear more—who I am if it doesn't come, or what will happen to me if it does.

If a cancer patient shows a clean bill of health for five years she is considered cured in the language of statistics. I always thought that a random number, and I find it somewhat ironic that it seems to have worked for me too. Five years almost to the day after Sally died I finally gave up the deathwatch I never should have embarked upon. I stopped with the yearly mammograms. I finally made a close friend.

Although Marilyn and I look so much alike that people take us for sisters, Marilyn's life is as different from mine as night is from day, and although we grew up in households that were fraught with the same kinds of anger, Marilyn reacted to hers in an entirely different way. As practical as the Volvo station wagon she carts her kids around in, Marilyn decided at twenty-one that babies were better than grad school, and anything was better than home. She married the first really decent man who asked her, and she had three kids in a row, the first so severely handicapped that the doctors said he wouldn't last a week and recommended that Marilyn save herself the heartache and just let him die.

But Marilyn had already had a lot of experience with heartache, so she took her son home and sang Fleetwood Mac songs to him—"Landslide" and "Silver Springs"—every night, and now he's twenty and has beaten the odds so many times the doctors have stopped saying anything at all. Marilyn's girls are smart and beautiful and on their way to boarding school at Exeter. Listening to her talk to them on the phone this week has been one of the very few things lately that has made me wish I had kids.

Marilyn doesn't find it nearly as astonishing as I do that she has made a marriage work for more than twenty years. She knows with absolute certainty that if her husband were to leave her, another man would want her. "It's got nothing to do with how we look or what we have to offer," she says as though it's a foregone conclusion. "Women like you and me radiate light."

Though Marilyn and her husband are well off, when I met her she'd never been off the eastern seaboard, scarcely out of New England even, and she doesn't really see that as a problem. I know she shakes her head every time she gets a postcard from me from God knows where.

We met on the Cape, and now we spend a week together there each summer. Last fall she came to France with me, and now she's here in Colorado at the ranch. I try to talk her into one trip after another—a weekend in New Orleans, a horseback trip in Ireland—and she just gives me a look that says I'm missing the point entirely.

I know that she's a little afraid that when I visit her house for the first time later this summer I'll see how domestic her life really is and it will send me running. She's as wrong about this as I'm wrong when I try to entice her with trips to somewhere faraway.

In spite of this, it was in France where my friendship with Marilyn solidified. I had taken a group of women writers there for ten days of writing and touring. Marilyn was my right-hand woman, her rent-a-Fiat keeping up with my rent-a-Citroën on the tight turns and corners, she and I going out at dawn each morning for croissants and orange juice, she giving the steering lessons when we canoed down the Dordogne. We were one bed short in the farmhouse we rented, so Marilyn and I shared the only queen.

We loved each other every minute of that trip, but neither of us are the type to go too far out there with our feelings. We got into bed each night like a couple of truckers, both in our ankle-length flannels.

"Nice driving, today," I'd say as I turned out the light, and she would say, "Same to you."

I wasn't with Sally on the day she died. It was February 8, a time when the light is returning, but so slowly that March 21 seems farther away than it really is. I was on a book tour, moving from city to city so fast that I could tell myself that the fact that I hadn't heard from Sally in over a week was more a function of my schedule than any real cause for alarm. When I got home to Utah I found out that no one else had heard from her the previous week either.

Sally had left her home, her husband, Ben, and her son, Eli, in Utah over a month before to follow a doctor to Tulsa, Oklahoma, who had given her faith in a highly experimental protocol. She had been staying at a motel there the whole time, but when I pressured the motel's receptionist he finally admitted that Sally had checked out over a week ago, and as far as he knew she'd gone to the hospital. The nurse said Sally wasn't taking calls, and when I begged them to let me talk to her roommate, she wouldn't tell me anything either. Finally a distant aunt of Sally's called me back in tears.

"I promised her I wouldn't tell anybody what was happening," she said, "but you have to come quick if you want to see her. It's a terrible thing," she said. "She's all blown up and yellow."

I called Ben and told him to pack a suitcase. Then I went to the ski area to find Eli and his snowboard on the slopes. At the airline counter the woman talked about bereavement fares and death certificates. "Oh, my mom's not going to die," Eli said, and that's when the concourse started spinning around me. Sally was the most honest and present person I had ever known, but the disease had taken that away from her. She was hiding from all of us, and part of me understood that was her privilege; the rest of me just hurt for Ben, and more than that for Eli, and most of all for myself.

We were still at the gate in Salt Lake City when the page came for Ben. The next few seconds were the least real part of it. The way Ben started crying first and then Eli, and then a man approached, only seconds later, as if from central casting, all in black.

"I'm a priest," he said. "Can I help?"

I didn't go with them. I stayed in Utah and watched their dogs and their horses, and picked them up at the airport when they brought her ashes home. I drove home from the airport alone that day into an early February twilight and then listened to my husband say how good it was that I wouldn't have to grieve. I didn't cry then, or at the funeral. What settled in me instead of grief was a slow and steady anger, and a wall that took five full years to come down.

I've written about Sally several times since she died, in both fiction and essays, but until now I've never even tried to write that airport scene. I'm in therapy now with a doctor that I trust more than any person I've ever known in my life.

Weeks after Marilyn's visit, as I begin to work on this essay, I will tell my therapist about finally getting to the airport scene and he will ask why I think it took me so long to write it.

I will talk about how writing changes an event forever; no matter how much I may try to record it accurately, once it is written it is subject to the alterations I have made, whether they are slight or major, and I can never trust my memory 100 percent after that. I will tell him that there are certain things about Sally that I haven't wanted to let go of, how I haven't wanted to let even something as personal as my writing interfere with my memory of certain events.

"What things about Sally were you trying to preserve in that way?" he will ask.

And, of course, it will be therapy, so my mind will race around like it always does trying to get the right answer. Surely the day at the airport can't be it, I will think, that day of negligence and bad timing and final and irreparable loss. Surely there are good things, happy things, I want to preserve, too, days before and even after she got sick when we were close and laughing and as in love as two heterosexual women can be. But hard as I will try to find a positive thought, my mind will just keep coming back to the scene at the airport.

"It's strange," I will say, tentatively, "but it seems like I have been trying to save that airport scene more than any other."

My therapist will get the stifled smile on his face that he reserves for moments just prior to a major breakthrough.

"And why do you think that would be?" he will say.

And then the truth will wash over me like a giant wave, and I will sit in his office and I won't be able to stop grinning. "Because there is value in the sadness," I will say, and his smile will be really uncontainable now. "It can fill you up," I will say, and I will mean it, "like happiness can, only in a different way."

We will sit quietly for a while, then, both of us watching the wheels in my head turn.

"It's just part of being alive," I will say, rolling now, saying things every healthy five-year-old knows and feeling wise beyond my years at the very same time. "And if sadness really doesn't kill you," I will say, "then you're home free in every situation. Then no emotional risk is too great."

Half the things on my worry Rolodex will be vanishing like thought bubbles. Maybe more than half. I will feel like I might elevate off the couch and start floating around the room.

"This might be a good place to stop for the day," he'll say, and I'll smile back at him.

"Good idea," I'll say, "we're sure not going to do any better than this."

We spent the first few days of Marilyn's visit in Denver, staying at the historic Oxford Hotel. I had big plans for us: massages, fancy dinners, clothes shopping, and pedicures.

Marilyn was very clear, however, that she didn't want anyone to touch her body, and what we wound up doing was walking around the city park talking until we were exhausted and then coming back to the Oxford for room service and a Fleetwood Mac concert on PBS.

We've been at my ranch house for five days now, and the days have taken on a rhythm of their own. We read in the morning, and if something occurs to us, we write a little. We march down the road to the creek like soldiers on a mission. We spend the heat of the day there throwing rocks, discussing fracture lines and strategies, getting soaked. We walk home satisfied, take turns in the claw-footed bathtub, cook something fresh and delicious to eat.

The strangest part of all this is that we've almost stopped speaking. It's not because we are mad, or even because we've run out of things to say to each other. It's something far better than that.

It's like the snowmelt and the lengthening days have simply taken ahold of us. Like we have tacitly agreed to accept the silence the mountains demand in this silent season. Summer is the time for talking, the mountains say, when the birds are singing and the creek is gurgling and there are leaves on the trees that will rustle in the wind. Now is the time to sit silently together, to feel the ice break around you, to wait for the first bluebirds to return to the feeder. Now is the time to heal.

Tomorrow the visit will be over, and I will take Marilyn to the airport. We will leave the house at four A.M. and will sing to the tape I made (Girl Songs, '98) most of the way. David, my wonderfully sensitive boyfriend who will have been sleeping in the backseat most of the way, will wake up just in time to try to get us to talk about how we feel about one another.

As we turn onto the ten-mile airport access road, Frederico Pena Boulevard, I will turn down the stereo. David will ask why, and I'll say, "In case any of us needs to make any closing remarks."

"Oh, like what," he'll say, "like you might want to say how happy you were that your friend came to visit you?"

I will think about what a beautiful thing the silence was between us. I will think of how it was the first time since Sally's death that I let ten days go by without doing any work.

"Yes," I will say, starting to blush, "in case we want to say anything like that."

"It was a great week," Marilyn will say quietly, and I'll agree, but that won't be enough for David.

"The two of you," he'll say, "two women who love each other so much and are still afraid to express their feelings."

I'll giggle uncomfortably, and Marilyn, who will be red to her ears will put her hands on her hips, turn full around to face him and say, "Look, David . . . we're fine."

It is a moment I will remember for its perfection. Two of the people I love most in the world being perfectly themselves.

And Marilyn will be right. We are fine. Whatever we say or don't say at the airport.

We've just spent ten days making spring come. From this day forward, the days will be longer than short.

TRAIL MIX

••

Lisa Price

Please God, help me—help me stay on the trail, help me to get back up each time I fall, help me find the emergency shelter that's supposed to be here.

I hear my whimpers and sobs with an odd detachment. Funny, this crying with no tears, but my tears have long drained, my eyes dry and chilled from the wind. I hear wailing deep in the wind, like distant calls from the ghosts of all those who have died up here on the way up Mount Washington.

The wind whacks me like a fire hose and reduces the physical act of hiking to the will to stagger to the next trail marker, a stripe of white paint on a cairn of rocks. The surrounding air moves so fast that it's hard to pull a breath. I kick toeholds in the frozen snowpack and take baby steps, but always the big gusts knock me down. I crawl for long periods of time on ridges, the wind yanking my backpack around to my side.

I'm in trouble, I understand that. I know I'm stumbling and

freezing, that I'm in over my head. I fight to focus my thoughts on the struggle, but I find myself thinking of Maude, the dog that traveled with me during four years of section-hiking portions of the Appalachian Trail.

Maude always nudged my leg when I stopped for breathers on long climbs or to figure out trail junctions. I'd lost her to cancer eighteen months ago. On this hike through New Hampshire and Maine, to the end-of-the-trail climb up Mt. Katahdin, I was on my own.

It is taking longer and longer to pick myself up from the snow. I find myself thinking of family and friends, seeing their faces. I'm sorry, I'm sorry, I tell them, but I just got so tired and cold. I tried for as long as I could. A dog would be blown off this mountain, I'm thinking, when the wind shuts off and I fall hard, finding myself in a lee of boulders.

I sit up and try to think straight. I'm so tired; this is so comfortable. I can't take the power and noise of the wind anymore. If I get in my sleeping bag, can I survive the night here? Can I make my fingers unzip my backpack? I've lost track of distance, and the sun is setting, I might not get to a better place. I stand up, I sit down, I stand back up. Get in the sleeping bag and see how it feels, I think, and I start to shrug out of the backpack.

A nudge on the leg, maybe it was just a finger of wind. No, another one, so I know for sure. I tuck my chin and step back into the wind, prompted by the spirit of Maude.

Fifty yards, maybe less, and I can see the building.

Thanks, Maude.

It's a thin line between bravery and ignorance, and I walked the tightrope through New Hampshire and southern Maine. The line is even thinner between determination and bullheadedness; in fact, I can never see it.

It's too early to hike up there, hiker friends had warned. You'll hit lots of snow and ice. And I'm hitting it, all right, usually with my face. Countless times every day, I'm walking on frozen snowpack when I suddenly break through, up to the knee, and I hear myself grunt as I land on the snow. But I can't just tuck my tail and go home, even if it's the smart thing to do.

The days blur and merge as I travel through the trackless white, and I start to get a little crazy. When the break-throughs fling me down I make frontal snow angels. Let those to come ponder these confusing tracks, I think.

A power plant lies on the Kennebec River somewhere above the trail crossing. Water is released on demand, not on a schedule, so hikers are advised to use the ferry service provided by the Maine section of the Appalachian Trail Conference.

I'm watching for something like a little tugboat with an engine, thinking the man in the red canoe is going fishing, but he turns out to be the ferry service. He paddles me across, just routine to him, but for me something changes on the north side of the Kennebec. Flowers like little red and white trombones are sprinkled through the woods on the opposite bank. The flowers announce that I made it. Everybody said I was crazy to hike through New Hampshire so early, but I did it.

I did not follow anyone else's tracks; I made my own.

The final section of the Appalachian Trail in Maine is called the 100-Mile Wilderness. Only two logging roads cross the trail in that expanse, so there's no place to resupply or get help.

For about sixteen years, hikers have stayed at Shaw's Boarding House in the town of Monson for a dose of hospitality before setting off into the wilderness. Two women from New Jersey drive up to Shaw's in the early evening and check in at the bunkhouse as I'm sorting my food.

One, Noel, hiked the trail to Monson in 1988, but it was late in the year, and the weather and disintegrating boots sent her home. The other, Caroline, has day hiked on the Appalachian Trail in Virginia.

"Hey," Mr. Shaw says, "you three should travel through the wilderness together."

We just look at each other.

I have my arm buried to the elbow in a big bag of chips, sticking the remaining shreds to my wet fingers and licking them off, burping a soda.

"Well," Noel says, "I can tell you're a hiker."

Hikers don't waste any food, especially junk food. I sense that Noel has had her share of chip binges. But I doubt that Caroline has ever experienced the bizarre food cravings of the trail-worn hiker, who eats pizza and ice cream with something approaching reverence. I knew Caroline wouldn't understand if I told her I'd walked ten miles round-trip on a paved road to buy Captain Crunch with Crunchberries.

So I don't commit. I just say that I'll start out with them in the morning. I figure that if they start to slow me down, I'll just make tracks.

Right from the start I'm chewing on the bit and fretting. Views of the trail are obliterated by Caroline's backpack, covered by a bright purple tarp and about three feet higher than her head. Squeezing it through the fallen trees is like trying to thread a sausage through a needle. She's making complete wardrobe changes with every change in terrain.

We walk for about two hours and stop for another break to eat lunch. Caroline estimates that we've gone about ten miles, and I'm nearly growling when I tell her, "It's more like three miles." She tells us how much her pack already hurts her shoulders and we compare pack weights. When we pack up to leave Noel carries Caroline's cold-weather gear, and I end up with her food bag.

"You know, with that goofy black hat, and all the duct tape patching your pants, and the string holding your boots together, you look like a scarecrow," Noel tells me. "That would be a good trail name for you."

Most hikers on the Appalachian Trail adopt trail names, nicknames usually chosen to coincide with occupations, physique, or style. My trail name is Dogless, I tell her grumpily, and walk along. My pack feels like a boulder, with the extra weight thumping on my back. I'm already planning how I'll say good-bye in the morning.

Later in the afternoon, when they turn and tell me they just realized that they haven't seen a trail marker for a while, I want to knock their heads together. We're lost for an hour, falling hard on rock ledges coated with flimsy moss, pushing our faces through wet, scratchy evergreens.

I'm in the lead when we get back on the trail but stop on the banks of Little Wilson Stream, mentioned in the guidebook with the notation "(ford)."

"This guidebook is messed up," Caroline says. "They should tell it like it is. This isn't a stream. It's a river with rapids."

Noel goes first, stepping carefully into the ice stream, leaning on her hiking stick. Caroline and I watch wordlessly as she inches her feet along the slippery bottom. The water level rises on her body: knees, hips, chest. Where the water is chest-deep it's sluiced between two rocks into an arching blast. In the sluice the current wrestles her, turning her, and as she fights it her hiking stick snaps. For several seconds she seesaws between balance and disaster, finally recovering and sloshing up onto the opposite bank, where she bends over in pain, her legs and feet cramping from cold damp and exhaustion.

Caroline, her face slack and pale, starts next, and we shout instructions over the noise of the water.

Undo your waist belt in case you fall; that way you can get out of your backpack easier. Slide your feet; don't lift them. Don't stare at the water. Don't take a step until both feet are set. Keep moving.

But Caroline stops moving in the sluice. She can't feel her feet. It's too cold. She can't move.

I'm busting through branches along the shore, hurrying to a point downstream where I might be able to snag Caroline if she falls. I miss seeing Noel go back in. When I get to the point I look upstream, and through a window in the trees all I see is the moment when their hands meet, Noel still cramped up and bent over, the water white-capping over her shoulders. That's the same moment I realize that a touch of two hands can defy definition. That's the same moment I realize there are ties stronger than any mountain torrent. That's the same moment I want to be their friend.

In the morning they ask me if I heard the UFO last night, and I start having doubts again. I eat, brush my teeth, and pack up while they're deciding what to have for breakfast. Caroline is braiding her hair and picking out a ribbon when I give up and set off alone, telling them I'll wait at the next ford.

Rushing water covers the stepping stones at Long Pond stream, but we decide we can use them if we take off our packs and pass them over. We shout our plan over the racket of the downstream waterfall. Noel steps carefully across, the water about knee-deep over the rocks. I go out to the first rock holding Noel's pack and wearing my own, the knifelike edge of the rock digging into my boot soles.

I fall in as I'm handing Noel the pack, and right away the water is tumbling me around. I can't tell where the top is, but I can hear that I'm headed for the falls. My heels bang a rock and I bicycle my legs, hoping for a grip. By then Caroline—hiker rookie, slow Caroline—has hurried to the top of the falls and is on her hands and knees in the turbulence. She snags me by the pack strap and drags me to waist-deep water.

And then I don't care if in the morning they tell me that they saw Elvis.

A day later Noel and I drop our packs for a rest near a lake, as Caroline catches up. We hear a large engine revving, and through the trees we can see shiny metal moving on the lake. We watch the clear spot at the end of a side trail to the shore, waiting to see what's making the noise.

"Look!" Noel shouts. "It's a plane!"

Caroline throws her pack on the ground and charges past us, pounding down the path as the plane turns and cranks its engine for takeoff.

"I have a VISA Gold Card," Caroline yells. "And I want out of here! I want a Diet Coke!"

The plane takes off as Noel and I roll on the ground in helpless laughter. And Caroline has christened herself with a trail name— Diet Coke.

● ●

Bogs, mountains, fords, bugs, roots, rocks, and so the days pass. We hike alone, in pairs, or as a trio. We talk for hours. We walk long hours in silence. Thirsty, cold, or tired in turns, we help each other through the hard times.

One afternoon I come upon an odd scene. There is Noel, one foot on a log, the other buried to the hip in muddy Maine muck. Caroline has her under one arm and is pulling, but they're both laughing too hard to make any progress. Noel sees me coming down the trail, and makes mock bug eyes of terror.

"Help!" she says, making her voice gravelly and strained. "The Swamp Thing's got me!"

Caroline and I yank Noel back and forth as the Swamp Thing emits ominous squishing and suctioning noises. Finally, with an earthen burp, her leg pulls free but with no boot. We have to dig for it. That night the boot rests like a trophy on a tall rock, drying by the campfire, a symbol of our tenacity.

I'm the only one of us who has a bug net to wear on my head, and Noel and Caroline ruthlessly tease me about its appearance, calling me names like Bride of the Wilderness, or the Veiled Threat. The next time I'm ahead on the trail, I plan a little performance wearing the bug net. I will be the Swamp Thing.

When I hear them coming up the trail I begin inching over a flat rock, growling in the Swamp Thing voice, "She walks, she talks, she crawls on her belly like a reptile."

It's a man and his son from Tennessee.

● ●

Despite the advice I gave her at the boardinghouse, Caroline insisted on bringing an outfit for every day, as well as loungewear for around the campfire. "Caroline," I'd said in Monson, "you just need two sets of clothes, one to hike in, and one to sleep in. That's why your pack is so heavy."

One night I'm in an outhouse when Noel knocks on the door. "Hurry up," she says, "you have to see this."

It's dark, but in the circle of firelight we see Caroline handling a system of sticks over the fire. She's burning her clothes.

I learn that Caroline is in the Service and will soon take her state boards to become a registered nurse. Noel is a professional photographer and martial arts expert, and she plans to attend college in the fall to become a physical education teacher. Those are the paths they plan to take, but who they are, their incredible substance, becomes more apparent as we make our tracks through the wilderness. I am proud to be ending my hike in the company of two women with such grit, humor, and generosity.

I've come a long way from that solo hiker who nearly welcomed the cold as an appropriate companion to fill the emptiness of my first Appalachian hike without Maude. I had spent many lonesome nights huddled in a sleeping bag on a shelf floor, a water bottle full of hot water held tight to my body. Now I've learned that we must fill our internal wilderness with people, and that sharing something—experiences, thoughts, food, care—with others is a truer, warmer way to live.

We have been seeing it for days now—Katahdin. Imposing, rising from the surrounding flatland, living justice to its Indian name, which means "greatest mountain."

Now, all too soon, we are at Katahdin Stream Campground at the base of the mountain, signing in at the ranger station before the ascent. In a notebook at the station many hikers have taken the time to sum up the jumble of thoughts facing them as they ended their hikes. So I want to take my time, to write something profound and inspiring for those to come.

"Five years of hiking this trail in sections is drawing to a close," I write. "But whether we realize it or not, the time and distance spent on this trail is just a small part of a greater hike each of us is on."

"Let's go," Noel says. "We've got a mountain to climb."

I look at the two of them. None of us has showered in a week. We are blistered and dirty; our clothes are muddy and torn. Suddenly we all grin at each other and pretty soon we're laughing, then we're crying, too.

In a hurry now, I turn back to the notebook.

"So consider all you have learned on this great adventure, face one another, and ask, how will you travel now?"

I tap the end of the pen on the page, thinking, as Noel and Caroline clump away down the steps, calling over their shoulders for me to catch up. I watch them cross the bridge to the trail, side by side, laughing about something, eating up the trail with eager strides.

"Share," I write, and hurry up the trail in their tracks.

THE FREEDOM MACHINE

••

Lucy Jane Bledsoe

On the day I met Barbara, Katie and I were doing some high-speed desert driving, me riding shotgun with my bare feet up on the dash, on our way to a trailhead in the Rockies. As always, we had promised ourselves that we would enter the Mojave in the early morning, even before dawn, but as always, delays in packing and eating, as well as general laziness, put us on the road about ten in the morning. Now as we drove the endless midday miles with the windows down, breathing the lung-scorching air, I concluded that we always leave later than expected because actually I like the desert at high noon; I love feeling stunned by its dragon's breath and lulled by the sight of its hallucinatory horizon.

"Can I turn on the air-conditioning now?" Katie asked just before noon.

"But don't you love the hot rush of air? The *real* air? How can we say we've experienced the desert if—"

"Okay, okay, okay."

Occasionally we passed an abandoned shack or trailer where people must have thought that given how cheap the land was, it was worth trying to survive here. I imagined their trips to Barstow for jugs of water, their afternoons—for surely they must have been unemployed to have chosen this for home—sitting limp in the thin wedges of shade cast by their shelters; I tried to guess how many days they hung in there before they gave up and quit. I admired these people who had tried this one last option, who had thought it might be better than urban homelessness, or moving in with the folks back in Wisconsin, or even just better than a mortgage. Following my lifelong habit of noting options, escape routes, lives I could live if I needed to live a different one, I put a mental Post-it on the Mojave Desert. I could live here if I had to. I could survive where others had not. I had skills.

At first I thought I was seeing a mirage: a shimmering on the highway ahead of us, sharp, steely flashes of metal and the wavering image of a human. As we drew closer I could have sworn it was a person on a bicycle, but it was high noon and we were eighty miles from the next town, a good twenty from the last one. It just didn't seem possible. Who would do such a thing? Then I laughed at myself: most people's mirages are bodies of water; mine are bicycles.

Ever since inheriting my first bicycle, an old, clunky yellow one-speed, I have been in love with two-wheelers. As a child I could get far from home in a matter of minutes, and while each mile away made me feel safer, endorphins nourished my imagination. On my bike, I learned that landscape is a continuum, that the city rolls right into the mountains. I learned that my body knows secrets my head does not know, secrets that could be imagined into stories.

Today the shelves of my writing room hold bicycle models, and the walls are covered with cycling posters. My favorite painting of all time is *Big Julie,* by Fernand Léger, which portrays a large, jaunty woman holding a flower in one hand and a mangled bicycle in the other. Butterflies flutter between Julie and her bike. Some people have totem animals; I have a totem machine.

That I might hallucinate a woman on a bike in the desert made perfect sense; however, as it turned out, this was no apparition. Before us was a real woman cycling across the Mojave Desert. We drew up behind the traveler and stared with disbelief at her long blond hair, the panniers on either side of her back wheel flapping open, revealing the clothing stuffed inside. Two smooth, varnished wooden sticks stuck out one of the panniers. She also had two Evian water bottles tied loosely to the stem of her saddle and they bonked against the panniers as she pedaled. The bike was a cheap-looking hybrid, the kind they give away if you spend over $300 at Sears.

The only explanation I could think of was that this woman was doing a story for *Outside* magazine: the Mojave Desert by bike, alone, in under eight hours. And for a moment I was over-whelmed with envy. I wanted out of our steel encasement. I wanted to feel the windblown sand in my face, the road grit under my tires. I wanted to taste the sage-flavored air, listen to the silence of the desert that is like no other silence. In other words, I wanted to move through this landscape slowly enough to engage all of my senses, but fast enough to experience exhilaration, which meant I wanted to do it on a bicycle. But . . . not on a cheap one like this woman's! Not with water bottles dangling off the saddle! Up close I saw that she had anything but an athlete's body; she looked doughy. This cyclist moved too slowly, and too joylessly, to be an adventure tourist.

It took a few moments for Katie and me to come to terms with the fact that this cyclist was real, not a figment of the desert's imagination. Then it took us another moment to decide that we should check out whether or not she wanted to be alone with her bicycle in the Mojave at noon. By then we had shot past the woman, but Katie made a U-turn and headed back. We passed the woman again, made another U-turn, then pulled alongside her.

I called out the passenger window, "Are you all right?"

She squinted at me.

"Need anything?"

"I could use a ride."

She definitely wasn't doing a story for *Outside* magazine. Katie pulled over and I helped the woman unload her panniers. We threw those in the backseat and put her bicycle on top of our backpacks in the far back. Then she crawled in next to her panniers, and we got a better look at her. Her long blond hair was tangled and dirty. The skin on her face looked as if it had burned and peeled a dozen times. She drained her Evian bottle, and we offered her water from our gallon jug. She refilled both of her Evian bottles, drank one down, and refilled it again, as if we might dump her back in the desert at any time, without notice. The only food we had in the car was PowerBars. She ate two in succession—a feat of true hunger—and took two more for later. We rolled up the windows and turned on the air-conditioning. My idea of playing at desert survival had suddenly lost its appeal.

Barbara could not, or would not, tell us where she was going, so we rode in silence for a while, feeling nervous and awkward. I surreptitiously checked the location of my wallet. Was this some kind of scam? Had we fallen into the hands of a highway con artist? But the devoured PowerBars and her sun-blistered face did not jibe with any possible scam I could think up.

Finally Katie and I began chatting to one another about our upcoming backpacking trip, trying to fill the awkward silence. Apparently our conversation eased her mind about us, and eventually she began asking questions about our trip. We in turn tried questioning her again and this time received answers. In fact, she opened up so completely we learned a great deal about her life and the purpose of her Mojave crossing by bicycle.

Barbara had been married for twenty years. Her husband had broken her arm twice, three ribs once, her jaw once, and had left her body covered with bruises more times than she could remember. He had prohibited her from ever leaving the house. If she did, and he found out about it, she got a beating. He also prohibited her from earning any money of her own and from having friends. The couple had two sons, the second of which had left home a month before the day we met Barbara. She had been waiting for that leave-taking for most of her twenty years of marriage. The same week her youngest son left, Barbara took his bicycle and panniers, which he had left in the garage, and made her escape one morning after her husband left for work.

The first hours were the most terrifying, she told us. She took only back roads, which lessened his chances of finding her, but the deserted, witness-free territory increased her chances of a more severe punishment if he did find her. By back roads it had taken her days just to get out of her home range. With each passing day she felt a little safer, though never completely safe.

Barbara hadn't the money to fly or to take a bus anywhere, but with the bicycle and enough cash to buy bread and peanut butter, she was making her way to a small town on the other side of the Mojave, the home of a childhood friend with whom she had not been in touch for years. Because her husband had doggedly recorded the addresses and phone numbers of all of her acquaintances, she had had to choose a friend and a destination he was not familiar with. This childhood friend did not know Barbara was coming. In fact, Barbara had told no one of her plans, not even her mother or sister, for fear that her husband would coerce them into giving him information, as he had done in the past.

By the time we met Barbara, she had cycled for twenty-four days and covered 600 miles. From the looks of her, the average of twenty-five miles a day would have been a full workout. She said that she usually slept in the heat of midday and rode mornings and early evenings. Occasionally she forked out the fifteen dollars to stay at a KOA campground, for the showers, but most often she slept in culverts. On the day we found her, she had begun to feel desperate. It was getting very hot, and she had seen no culverts, no shade, no hiding places. It was as if she had been oblivious to the fact that the highway she was following had entered a desert.

As I stared out at the unending two-color tableau of sand and sky and listened to Barbara, a new wave of envy blew through me. I thought it crude to envy a woman who had been forced to escape an abusive relationship by means of a grueling physical journey of another kind. But she was, in fact, *making the journey*. She was running away. She was claiming her own path, and doing it with a bicycle. I envied her for having the guts.

For all of my life, as far back as I can remember, I have longed to be somewhere else. Somewhere wilder. Somewhere warmer. Somewhere with more heart. As a child, though I couldn't actually leave home altogether, I found temporary escape on my bicycle. Riding hard—until the sweat ran down my back, until my lungs felt like bursting—scoured out my confusion and pain, and delivered me to a bright place of contentment. Today I still try to ride to that place. Getting on my bicycle is synonymous with saying, *I'm outta here.* If I'm lucky, ten or twenty miles into a ride, escape, wilderness, and freedom combust together and burn off my fear. On my bicycle I can arrive at places of great courage.

Yet just as I play at desert survival with mind games in the car, or even during backpack trips of a few days' duration, my escapes by bicycle have been child's play compared to Barbara's use of the freedom machine.

I tried to tell her how courageous I thought she was.

But she only shrugged and said that the bicycle ride across the mountains and desert didn't scare her half as much as her marriage had. In fact, though she told stories of difficulties on the road, she preferred talking about her traveling triumphs. Her favorite story was about the time she was ascending a mountain pass and came to a road sign announcing that the road from that point on was closed. Unable to imagine turning back, she continued forward until she came to the place where a road crew was clearing a huge rock slide. She hoisted her bicycle and carried it across the rubble to the amazement, and eventual admiration, of the road crew. They applauded her when she finally reached the other side of the long stretch of broken rock. About five times she told us about that applause, and I realize now that it must have sustained her across much more than the debris of one rock slide.

I have spent several years thinking about Barbara and her story. Her appearance in my life has felt mythic, a backward- and forward-looking message that I couldn't decipher. At first unwilling to look at the personal significance of her journey to me, I began trying to understand by placing it in a historical context.

When the bike craze hit the United States at the end of the nineteenth century, women immediately saw this new machine as a vehicle of emancipation. In 1895, Frances Willard, the temperance leader and suffragette, wrote an entire book called *A Wheel Within a Wheel* on how the bicycle and cycling serve as the perfect extended metaphor for the feminist cause, indeed, for all things important in life, from health to politics. Willard grew up on the prairie and spent her childhood romping in the out-of-doors. She insisted on wearing her hair short, which was very unusual for a girl at that time, and on being called Frank. She wrote that she "ran wild" until her sixteenth birthday, at which time she was forced into long skirts, corsets, and high heels. Though she spent most of her adult life working for temperance and women's suffrage, she did not feel that she truly regained her personal freedom until 1893, when at the age of fifty-three she learned to ride a bicycle. Willard equates a woman's mastering of the bicycle with her mastering control of her personal destiny, and claiming her own path.

Susan B. Anthony agreed, saying that bicycling gave women "a feeling of freedom and self-reliance," and that a woman on a bicycle is "the picture of free, untrammeled womanhood." Anthony claimed that bicycling did "more to emancipate women than anything else in the world."

As more and more women took to "the wheel," manufacturers began making bicycles and other cycling products especially for women. The Starley Brothers made the first mass-produced women's bike, the "Psycho Ladies' Bicycle," and other manufacturers came up with products to battle the prevalent idea that cycling ruined a woman's femininity. One company invented a screen that, once attached to the bicycle, blocked the view of a lady's ankles and feet.

Even with such precautions, female cyclists were scorned in the dominant media. The proliferation and vehemence of newspaper and magazine editorials lambasting women cyclists proved that men were quite aware of the bicycle's role as a tool for gaining freedom. Some wrote that the freedom felt on a bicycle might intoxicate women to the point that they would want, perhaps even demand, other freedoms. Others believed that the shape of a bicycle seat might stimulate a woman in immoral ways. Groups even lobbied to have bicycles outlawed for women. These pundits warned that on a bicycle a woman had no need of an escort. Though the logic of this fear is difficult to grasp—Did she not need an escort because she could now out-pedal dangerous encounters?—it is easy to see how the idea of women not needing men would severely challenge the status quo. In 1895, in the *Minneapolis Tribune,* Ann Strong stated that bicycles were "just as good company as most husbands," and better yet, when a woman was tired of her bicycle, she could "dispose of it and get a new one without shocking the entire community." The Victorian era, along with many of its strict rules intended to protect women's femininity, was on its way out. For some women, Margaret Valentine Le Long, for example, the end of the era couldn't come quick enough. In 1896 Le Long ignored her family and friends who begged her to stay home, and she rode her bicycle, alone, from Chicago to San Francisco, wearing a skirt and carrying a pistol.

I wonder what Barbara of the Mojave would have to say about Willard's book and theses, about Anthony's declaration, about Le Long's armed trek across two thirds of the continent. For Barbara, the bicycle meant freedom in its most literal form, physical survival, and perhaps the urgency of her journey was too great for her to be able to reflect on her place in the history of women, bicycles, and freedom. But *I* could reflect on these topics, and it helped me to begin to understand the personal significance of the intersection of Barbara's path and my own.

●●

As it turned out, we had found Barbara on the last leg of her journey. The next town, or so she told us, was her destination. As we drew closer to the home of her childhood friend, her thoughts turned to finding work. She thought her friend would welcome her, but for how long? She had to find work, which would be very difficult since she hadn't held a job in twenty years. She spoke with pride of the one-woman gardening business she had had before her marriage. Although most of her tools were long gone, she carried in her panniers a large pair of clipping shears, which she talked about almost as much as she talked about the road crew's applause. I guessed that that one pair of shears was her only reminder of her skills, of her independence, of her ability to take care of herself.

Barbara didn't know the exact location of her friend's house and told us to drop her off at a gas station in town. As we pulled off the highway to let her out, I imagined that it was I who was getting ready to begin a new life here. The air was dusty hot, and the few buildings looked more like children's forts, with boards nailed roughly together, than bona fide establishments. The homely starkness attracted me. Perhaps I could hide from other people here, but I could never hide from myself. Where could I go? One step out the door and it would be me, sand, and sky. Maybe the desert, even this weather-beaten town, wasn't the last resort I had earlier assumed it to be. Maybe it was a first resort. Maybe it was the beginning.

"Will you be okay?" I asked Barbara, meaning, did she feel safe from her husband? and perhaps meaning, could she find her friend's house? But she cast her eyes over the few businesses in that tiny dry town and said something about finding work. "A waitressing job, maybe," she said, "but without any experience . . ." It was as if we didn't even exist anymore. She had escaped her hometown, tackled the Sierras, the desert, and now she turned without pause to the next obstacle. I guessed that over the last twenty years she had had a lot of practice in living life like a video game, clearing one obstacle and immediately bracing herself for the next one.

I told her that I hoped there would be some sensible employer in town who would realize that riding a bicycle 600 miles, over the Sierras and across the Mojave, said a lot more about a person's character and capabilities than previous experience serving bacon and eggs. She smiled and said she hoped that was the case. We gave her the rest of our PowerBars and some cash.

As Katie and I drove away, we were silent for a few minutes, and then we admitted to one another that we were trying to find flaws in Barbara's story, again wondering if she could be some kind of highway con artist. But as hard as we tried, we could think of no way that a woman riding a bicycle alone across a desert could be a con. In fact, our searching for an explanation other than the one Barbara gave us was absurd. Domestic violence is as common as dirt. What was uncommon was Barbara's courage, her willingness to cross the severest of geographical landscapes to overcome the personal landscape of her life.

The truth is that when I met Barbara out there in the middle of the Mojave, I already knew her. She was the literal embodiment of all that the bicycle has meant to me: escape from home; physical empowerment; and, ultimately, a rediscovery of my imagination in landscape.

NATURAL ORDER

••

Amy Irvine

I have never been a hunter, though all the men in my family—and even a few of the women—are. As a pot of evening tea brews on my camp stove, I ponder this thought and watch a coyote move through the long lavender shadows cast by the Teton range onto Lupine Meadows. He has his nose to the ground and lopes in circles, directly beneath Mount Teewinot. The meadows are now the tired gold color of summer's end and camouflage the predator well. He slows his movement and crouches low. I can tell he has found a scent and is stalking a creature much smaller than he—a field mouse most likely, but perhaps a golden-mantled squirrel. Pouring the tea, I follow the coyote's movements in the fading light, then grip my mug tightly as the anticipation of the hunt builds.

The pounce is catlike and sudden. I admire the wild dog's powerful body as he springs out of the brush into the air. Yarrow and sage shiver as the coyote settles down for its meal. I imagine the rodent's last breath and its small, dark marble eyes looking into those of its captor. I am sad for the creature, though I understand that this is the natural order of things. And despite my hunting heritage, I realize I have come to identify with what it is like to be prey.

Witnessing the coyote's hunting ritual marks the beginning of my own rite: an annual retreat to Grand Teton National Park to watch the folding of summer into autumn. I have spent summers here since I was a young girl, visiting my uncle who for over thirty years worked as a climbing ranger at Jenny Lake, home of the Tetons' climbing and rescue rangers. In my twenties I learned to climb on the granite walls and snowfields of this range. I have come up here every year since then with different climbing partners to test my skills on various routes and peaks. Always I have come to this place driven by the fear that I won't measure up as the niece of a legendary climbing ranger; I come from a family that rates its members' worth by physical prowess, self-sufficiency, and ability to face danger. And one has points automatically deducted for being female. Perhaps this male-identified family system fuels my need to return year after year, to test my mettle on these remote rock faces.

Now, as a woman of thirty-one years, I have returned to these mountains without a partner. Only my journal, a small pair of binoculars, and water bottles will accompany me. This year's plan is to wander the Teton range slowly, to savor its canyons, through which I usually rush on my way to conquer some summit. This year I want no agenda, for other agendas have quickly filled the once wide and easy spaces of my life: a serious job, a marriage, a mortgage payment. This year, too, I want no danger. Life seems stressful enough. Most of all, I want solitude.

But as the pastels of twilight collapse into a dark night sky, I know I am not alone. Indeed, a woman has accompanied me, and although her presence is only figurative, her sad fate has rooted itself firmly in my mind and will accompany me, like a shadow, up into the Tetons.

This morning I left Salt Lake City and its desert heat and headed north in my new Toyota van—a symbol of the conventional and upwardly mobile course my life has been on of late. In comparison to all of my previous vehicles, this van's features are luxurious; the hood of one former car was tied down with nylon climbing rope—and its floor had rusted through so badly that I could see pavement. Given my history with cars, my pleasure over my new van's cruise control, captain's chairs, and air-conditioning was considerable. Most thrilling to me was the sleeping space I created by replacing the back passenger seats with a futon mattress, so I could travel alone and sleep safely at night. I drove with my big toe just reaching the gas pedal; because I am a small woman I have been warned that the air bag in the steering wheel, if deployed, could kill me. I have been told I should ride in the backseat like a child . . . to be safe.

Utah's basin and range gave way to Wyoming's high plains. I hit the sleepy town of Afton and made my way to a convenience store for a cold drink. In the parking lot was an old Dodge pickup; its engine idled roughly. As I walked by, three young men with sunburned necks leaned out the windows and whistled in a slow, low fashion that made me wish I were wearing a looser-fitting shirt. I hurried inside.

Arriving in Jackson around four o'clock in the afternoon, I stopped for gas before heading out to the park. I waited by the pump, arms wrapped around my chest to protect me from the cool

Wyoming air. Looking up, I met the steel-gray eyes of a cowboy. His gaze was hard and cold, making my skin prickle. Again, I found myself hurrying inside.

This time my hand stopped on the gas station door. Plastered on its glass was a cotton-candy pink flier bearing the photo of a young woman's face. The word MISSING sat squarely above her smile. I knew about this woman. Though I didn't know her personally, she and her husband are part of Wyoming's outdoor community—my community. Many of my friends know the couple well; the woman is a terrific trail runner, and they are both climbers. I heard from our mutual friends that she was running in the hills above Lander, Wyoming, not far from the Tetons, when she vanished into the mountain air, leaving behind her car, her wallet and keys. As I begin this trip, she has been missing for three months.

She was staring back at me from the flier, which had been generously circulated by the outdoor community throughout the Rocky Mountain states. Her sweet, youthful face felt so proximate to my life; she has hiked and run and climbed in the same mountains with the same people that I have, and she has often done these things alone, as I have in the past, as I am now. This knowledge has haunted me since I first saw the flier in an outdoor shop in Salt Lake. As I embarked upon a solo trip that would include hiking alone in the backcountry, the fate of this missing woman settled heavily on my shoulders. We share the same name—Amy.

Long after my uncle retired from his post at Jenny Lake, I find I am still in the habit of staying with Jenny Lake rescue rangers. They have the best accommodations of anyone in Jackson Hole: the park's management houses them in Lupine Meadows, away from the tourists, in cabins that were built in the 1930s—complete with crooked wooden porches that face the jagged Teton peaks. Besides, many of the rangers have been my climbing mentors and friends over the years, and it is a special occasion to return from a day in the mountains and spend an evening with them. Jenny Lake rangers always have a jug of wine on hand, riveting stories to tell, and sage advice to impart to those of us with less experience in the tempestuous Tetons.

This year I am staying at Tom Kimbrough's place. The cabins are small, so I set up camp outside, venturing inside only for water and bathroom privileges. After finishing my tea and leaving Tom with a small gift of tomatoes—the last from my garden for the season—I bid the coyote in the field good-night and make my bed in the back of the van. For a while I lie with the side door open, listening to the elk bugling across the meadow. The moon illuminates the bats crawling from the eaves of Tom's cabin. Their vast numbers and erratic flight patterns amaze me. I close the van door. With a click of one small button, the entire van automatically locks each of its doors and activates an alarm system. I feel safe in this new car of mine, but unnaturally so.

Still, I do not sleep. The face of the missing woman, named Amy Roe Bechtel, comes to me. Questions about her fate prowl around my imagination throughout the night: She was strong, healthy, able-bodied. I know from her poster that she was small like me—we share roughly the same height and weight. She, too, might have been urged to sit in the back of my van to be safe from its airbags. I wonder how much her size, and sex, accounted for her becoming prey . . . for that is what I now presume happened to her.

I know the authorities think it unlikely that Amy was dragged off by a cougar or a bear. Nor did she tumble from a cliff; searches for her have revealed nothing. It is more likely that she was overtaken by a man, or men, who probably had a vehicle and a weapon. I wonder, did she try to run? Surely her strong legs and lungs would have given her a shot at escape. Did they trick her by stopping to ask for directions? Where was she taken? Did she feel small and weak and helpless, in spite of her strong body? I play out scenarios, luridly. I imagine her face as her predators closed in on her. Unlike the coyote hunt I witnessed earlier this evening, this, I think to myself, is not the natural order of things. Surely we are not meant to be preyed upon by our own species.

I beg for sleep to come and draw a veil over Amy's face, which stares in at me through each van window. I had so much looked forward to a peaceful trip, one without danger, one during which I wouldn't need to prove anything to a climbing partner, to my uncle and the other men in my family. But Amy's presence in my mind changed everything.

The following morning I load up my daypack and head to the Jenny Lake boat dock. My plan is to take the boat across the lake to Cascade Canyon, which carves out the north side of the Grand Teton and Mount Owen. At the dock I meet my friend Pete Lenz, an emergency doctor from Salt Lake, and Peter Lev, who directs the park's guiding service. They are loaded down with enormous packs, outwardly decorated with helmets and ropes. The two men plan to hike in and climb Table Mountain the following day. Since we are headed in the same direction, they invite me to hike with them for a while. The two Petes and I roam along the stream beneath a verdant Valhalla Canyon, which reclines between the peaks high above us. We then pass under the elegantly fierce north face of the Grand Teton. Swapping climbing tales and bear stories, each of us tries to outdo the others in hyperbole. Although I had planned to hike alone, I delight in their company after such a restless night.

We stop for lunch at the turnoff to Lake Solitude, and by now the two Petes are quizzing me about my agenda for this Teton trip. This is requisite for climbers' conversation: the sharing of what routes one plans to do and with what gear and in how much time. I tell them I am not climbing this trip. Explaining my original desire to wander these mountains without adrenaline-fed goals, I admit, morbid as it may be, my newly emerging need to contemplate the fate of the missing woman from Lander. I feel vulnerable, sharing my fears that a similar fate might befall me on one of my solo excursions.

I expect to draw semi-blank looks or even smirks from these men, since I feel that my thoughts are teetering on the brink of obsession and paranoia. But both men take me seriously. Pete Lenz, who works as an emergency medical practitioner in an urban setting, responds that carrying a gun may not be a bad option for me to consider. Peter Lev's face is one of a father. "My eleven-year-old girl has seen those MISSING posters all over Jackson," he says. "She finally said to me, 'So I have to watch out for bad guys in the mountains, Dad?' I am sick that when she comes out here"—Peter spreads his arms wide as if to gather the entire Teton range in his arms—"and she'll be forced to think about this sort of thing."

In the afternoon I wish my friends good luck on their climb and return to Tom's cabin. That night I dream I am a young girl again. With my little sister and cousin, I am camped in a tent outside my uncle's cabin in Lupine Meadows. I am sitting up in my red flannel sleeping bag and looking out at the cabin, in which our parents and other family members sleep. Wooden shutters are closed over the cabin's windows as they are in the winter, when the structure is vacant. Suddenly, the shutters fly open and the men in my family—my father and his brothers and my male cousins—are standing there with guns drawn. They begin shooting from the window, past the tent in which I sit. I stick my head out to see what they are shooting at: I see ten beautiful black bears dancing on their hind legs. Blood runs off their coats and pools in the sage and dirt. One by one the bears fall. My sister and cousin jump out of their sleeping bags, join hands, and in their nightgowns dance in a circle, singing, "No bears are out, that's right. Daddy shot them all tonight!" I run to help the bears but they are dead. Their shiny black eyes stare straight up at the moon.

The following morning over tea, Tom and I discuss how carrying a gun changes one's consciousness. Tom tells me how he refused to pack a weapon when the Park Service arranged for the Jenny Lake rangers to obtain their police commissions. I tell Tom about a night on the Green River when I was eight years old and some barefoot crazy man wearing only blue jeans and tattoos walked into our camp and pulled a knife on my mother. I tell him how frightened I was when my father turned a pistol on the guy and chased him away. Tom asks which scared me more—the idea that the guy could actually hurt us or the thought that my father would use the gun on him. I say I don't know. What I do know is that I can't imagine Amy Roe Bechtel running a mountain trail with a gun in her hand.

As I pack up my gear for a day in Paintbrush Canyon, a backcountry ranger named Goldie stops by and asks if he can join me since he's going that way. I accept, and it is not lost on me how comforting it is to have the company of protective male figures like mountain guides and doctors and rangers as I hike these trails. As I leave, Tom comes out of his abode and hands me a can of pepper spray, which many people carry in the backcountry in case of a bear encounter. In cities now, people also carry it for self-defense, instead of Mace. Ironically, the writing on the can says NOT FOR USE ON LARGE ANIMALS. Tom, Goldie, and I laugh that I could use it to ward off mosquitoes.

Goldie is good company, naming obscure wildflowers and pointing out geological history I couldn't have guessed at. He teases me about being the perfect size for mountain lion prey, and tells me I should watch my back on the trail. I thank him for adding to my anxieties and leave him at Holly Lake, where he'll stay the night. I hope to cover the six miles back to the trailhead before dark, but I have gone farther than I had expected to in the abbreviated daylight hours of early autumn, and my ankle is sore from a light sprain suffered a few weeks earlier.

The sun is low and the trail empty. I sing and make up nonsense rhymes, partly to warn any sow bears with cubs that I'm in the vicinity, but also because the silence that fills the canyon—the same silence that only a short time ago was so delicious to share with my hiking companion—now feels tense and unnatural, as if the air could shatter.

When I hit the tree line the forest is thick and full of deep blue shadows. I am irritated with myself for being so fearful of the gift of solitude. Voices inside call me a coward and a child, tell me I should just stay home behind locked doors if this is how I'm going to behave. The trail is quickly losing its definition in the waning light. My ankle turns on sharp jutting stones. I stumble on tree roots and jump at the sound of the wind hissing across tree boughs. The critical voices are a rancorous chorus now, and a glimmer of panic begins to command my coordination and logic.

There are three miles to go. They are long miles, and I fail to notice things I had admired on the way up the canyon that morning—the dish-sized mushrooms and diaphanous white columbine that should have finished blooming long before now. Finally I hit the switchbacks, signaling the last stretch above String Lake, which I must then circle in order to reach my van at the trailhead. It is nearly dark now on the front side of the Teton range. My joints hurt from moving downhill so rapidly, and I slow down in spite of myself.

A tall figure appears at the opposite end of the switchback. He moves toward me, with a bold, powerful stride. Strangely, my mind ticks through a list of things to do when encountering a bear. Stand still. Don't make eye contact. Throw it your pack. Play dead. Climb a tree. I think of the dancing bear dream.

Next: the pepper spray will only work on small animals.

And then: Stay calm. Keep moving with an air of confidence and a sense of purpose. Make direct eye contact. Look tough.

Act like a man.

With head up and shoulders back, I mirror the man's stride. It is only when he is three feet from me that I can see his face. It is a stern face, with a bushy, unkempt beard. He is wearing heavy work boots and pants, and a flannel shirt. There is a knife sheathed in his belt. He looks like a lumberjack.

Or a hunter.

Now he's directly in front of me; I can just see his eyes. I see, too, that he carries a flashlight, which is not yet turned on. He stops. I feel my body lift from the ground and move laterally to the other side of the trail.

He speaks. I expect a throaty growl, but he says, "How do you do?" in a gentle, fluid tone, like water moving over stones.

"Fine," I stammer, trying to sound confident.

He takes a step toward me. I jerk backward, falling into the slope on the uphill side of the trail. Arms and legs are everywhere, and I can't tell if they are only mine or someone else's too. Through my head an old, grainy reel of film spins into fast motion. I see at lightning speed the scenario I have orchestrated of Amy's demise: She is running, muscles rippling across her legs as her feet strike dirt. The sun casts bright light off her blond hair. The pickup slows to a crawl, and as she turns to look over her shoulder a large, backwoods-looking man jumps out and grabs her from behind. The image flickers and blurs here, as his meaty arms wrap around her waist and lift her from the ground, her legs dangling like a doll's.

Next I see stories from recent newspapers, bleeding from black-and-white words into images of gray: For ten days, two women were stalked on the Appalachian Trail then viciously murdered in their tent. Another woman, an Olympic biathlete, was abducted while training on a mountain trail, dragged away by two men to a remote cabin. She was held captive for two months, as the "wife" of the younger man. A Utah woman was running in Millcreek Canyon, a place where I hike in the evenings after work. She was struck down by a car. The driver then assaulted her on the roadside gravel. When the man was captured a few days later, it was discovered that he had a history of randomly taking out his rage on women. The final image I see is one of my mother and grandmothers and aunts, standing at the door of our home, calling to me to come inside.

Then I see my feet and hands grasping at anything for balance, finding only slick, decomposing foliage and fecund soil. Whimpering, helpless sounds escape from my throat. The man on the trail before me takes a step back, the darkness eclipsing his face.

"I'm sorry, ma'am. Didn't mean to scare you." He sounds confused. "I was looking for my wife. She came up here this afternoon while I was fishing Cottonwood Creek, and she hasn't come back yet."

I struggle to my feet and mutter a garbled band of words that make no sense to either of us. I scuttle around the tall man like a wild animal and break into a run. I run the remaining miles, and Amy is next to me, her footsteps pacing mine, her breath guiding mine, in and out, in a controlled, practiced rhythm. I do not stop until I reach my van.

The next day I am at the ranger station, saying good-bye to Tom. I see the man from the Paintbrush Canyon trail with his wife. They explain that she had chosen to hike another trail, and had experienced no difficulties other than returning late to their camp. The man apologizes for scaring me on the trail, and I redden with embarrassment.

Leaving Jackson I strain for one last glimpse of the Tetons in my rearview mirror. Passing through Hoback Junction and then following the sinuous curves of the Snake River, I spot four-wheel-drive vehicles parked in clusters at trailheads that lead into the National Forest bordering the other side of my route. It is the beginning of hunting season. I think of the men in my family, and a few of the women, who are undoubtedly out today in woods like these, weapons slung over their shoulders, red-faced and smiling in the cool fall air as they look for their prey. I think of the coyote in Lupine Meadows. I think of Amy Roe Bechtel, and I know I will never again wander in the wilderness without her, without her fate shaping the way I view the shadows and hear the sounds along the trail. Then I adjust my captain's chair, take my big toe off the gas pedal, and set my cruise control at a safe and comfortable fifty-five.

TO THE LAKE

• •

Bridget Quinn

Unfortunately, one only remembers what is exceptional. And there seems to be no reason why one thing is exceptional and another not. Why have I forgotten so many things that must have been, one would have thought, more memorable than what I do remember?

—Virginia Woolf, "A Sketch of the Past"

It began strangely: Thunderstorms in the morning.

I woke up early to run and it was raining, though in July rain usually isn't something to stop you from running. For weeks the air had been heavy with a combination of moisture and heat I never knew before moving to the East Coast, the kind of humidity that makes you equally wet running without rain as in it. Both experiences are distinctly unrefreshing. New York summer rain isn't cool, it's warm. For those of us from the West—where rain in summer is enough of an anomaly—it's a strange and unsettling experience, like entering some mixed-up unnatural circle of hell.

It wasn't until I saw the lightning from our bedroom window, great cracks out of a heavy gray sky above the Shawangunk ridge, and heard the following rumbles echoing across the valley that I decided not to run. I spent the next hour sitting on the porch steps with my husband, sipping thick coffee he'd boiled on the stove, calming our quivering dogs and enjoying the strange spectacle of morning lightning in July through a heavy downpour of warm rain.

When it stopped the transformation was sudden and complete, the sky bursting open blue, the sun breaking out bright and blazing hot. The radio said it would be over 100 degrees again, and I wondered what to do with myself. It was too hot to stay home and too hot to do anything. Then the phone rang. It was Teri inviting me on a ride with her and Susie. It seemed insane in the brutal heat, but I wanted to go. I felt like the coolest girls in school had asked me to their party, and though I might be nervous about measuring up (was I cool enough? cute enough? fit enough?), not going would mean admitting my utter hopelessness. And what if I was never asked again?

I had half an hour to get ready, time many people (read: men) would probably spend tuning their bikes, making sure every part was fitted, filled, greased. A flat or broken chain on a day so stifling would be miserable, possibly dangerous. I gave my bike a good long glance and it looked fine to me. I located helmet, sunglasses, sunscreen, then filled two water bottles and stuffed a couple of energy bars and a banana in a fanny pack. Total, bike prep took approximately seven minutes. Then I worked on myself. I took a shower, slicked back my hair, and tried on different pairs of bike shorts. I opted for short green ones which, though they risked revealing a less than perfectly well-toned area of upper thigh to my absurdly buff friends, were cotton. Vanity wasn't worth heat stroke or an incipient yeast infection. Not quite.

But even so, I checked myself in full bike regalia in the bedroom mirror before leaving. I needed different socks. I opted for a pair that were thinner, therefore cooler, which was important, but more crucially, they were white, making my pale legs look maybe a subtle shade darker.

I wanted to look good for my girlfriends. Or it might be more honest to say, I wanted to look good to them. I don't think it's about attraction per se, the way it might be around men, but a sort of competition, albeit a subtle and hard-to-admit one. I wanted to look as good as they did. At least as good. No one wants to think of themselves as being that shallow, but there you are.

Here is the irony of venturing outdoors in the company of women: rather than feeling less intimidated than I would with men, I was far more aware of my shortcomings as an outdoorswoman and athlete. What if I couldn't keep up? I was mortified at the thought of Susie and Teri dragging me through the ride, waiting for me at the top of hills. Of my slowing them down and destroying their pleasure. And as I stood in the tall grass of Susie's driveway, waiting for Teri to pull up, I also realized with horror that I didn't know how to fix a flat tire or how to perform even basic bike maintenance. Since I usually rode with my husband (a bike mechanic), I'd never thought much about it. But when he pulled my bike off the roof rack then handed me a patch kit, I realized that if I flatted I'd have to ask Teri and Susie for help.

I knew they could tackle a flat or anything else, because, unlike me, they seemed to be sure and competent outdoorswomen. In addition to being accomplished rock climbers, runners, bikers, and who knew what else, they went to Colorado together every winter for a few weeks of backcountry skiing, hut to hut, in remotest, high-altitude avalanche country. I love Nordic skiing, but I learned as a high-school exchange student in Norway, where skiing is less an adventure than a pleasant communal holiday enjoyed among neighbors and friends. I wouldn't know the north end of a compass, much less how to navigate heavy powder between two unrelated points on a distant mountain. I had never set up my own tent, started my own stove, waxed my own skis. The list was endless and shameful.

But once we got on our bikes my insecurities gradually dropped away with the steady push and pull of my legs on the pedals, the even rush of my heavy breathing, and the concentration of keeping my eyes on the steep trail. We rode together, as a pack, sometimes talking, often not. There was no one waiting for me, no one literally pushing my butt to help me climb faster, no one circling back to see how I was doing. There were three of us keeping a steady pace, and it struck me that for the first time in my adult life, I felt physically strong.

The ride wasn't an easy one. Our route consisted of two hours of almost steady climbing, from Susie's house to our destination at the cool haven of Lake Awosting in Minnewaska State Park. Under normal circumstances it was a long, hard push. In the brutal heat, it was a possibly foolish undertaking.

We weren't racing and no one was pushing to outride the others, but we weren't taking it easy either. Even on the worst uphills, we kept spinning evenly. I was proud, even amazed, to be keeping up and felt exhilarated by the sense of combined effort, by the simple joys of speed and camaraderie. It reminded me of riding bikes as a kid, tearing around the fields with my friends, unaware of anything but the pure pleasure of navigating on two thin wheels at as high a speed as possible. Then, as on this day, there was no objective. It was just fun, riding for the uncomplicated delight in movement and physical exertion.

No part of our route could be considered technical. There was no singletrack, for example, and only short rock-strewn or root-infested sections to navigate. But the climbing could be torturous and the descents dangerous, with switchback after switchback, often on totally blind turns along precipitous cliffs. The ride primarily followed one of the old carriage trails carved out in the nineteenth century to take fashionable Hudson Valley visitors on tours through the remarkable landscape of an area that is still wild and reasonably pristine a hundred years later.

The trail we chose wound through meadows of long grass, pale green in the bright sunshine, beneath a shocking blue sky. But the relief of riding a section of flat was outweighed by the intense heat of little shade. Suddenly there was sweat dripping from under my helmet and into my eyes. My lips, I realized, were frosted with salt and my mouth felt simultaneously sticky and dry. I had a momentary urge to whine, but checked myself. Neither Susie nor Teri looked particularly joyous at this juncture either, but they weren't complaining. I pulled my water bottle out of its cage and took a long swallow of lukewarm liquid. It was the opposite of satisfying, a tantalizing taste of what should have been, but wasn't. I sprayed some directly onto my face and chest, and that was marginally more refreshing.

Just as heat exhaustion seemed imminent, the trail turned upward again and reentered a more forested section, providing intermittent shade. In addition to welcome shelter from the sun, the trail traveled miles along sheer drop-offs, literally cliff edges, where one wrong move would send you plummeting several hundred feet before you met earth again. The vistas from these precarious sections are particularly thrilling—the Hudson Valley rolling out for thousands of acres in every direction, like an overawing picturesque landscape by some nineteenth-century Romantic painter. Except this was real, a sublime fantasy of grandeur and majesty extending from the view out there, right up to the ground beneath our knobby tires. I had to remind myself not to get too captivated by the sweeping view, to keep my eyes on the trail, so as not to end up one of the inevitable yearly statistics of grisly mountain-bike misfortune. Fortunately, the trail itself was inspiring, lined with pink and white mountain laurel perfuming the air as we sped through, and, underneath, the azure and indigo accents of wild blueberries.

On one steep section we passed an ancient gazebo of gnarled and bent wood, bolted to the living rock at the lip of the cliff. Susie pointed it out—it was nearly hidden by a shelter of trees just behind it. I'd never noticed this gazebo before, though I'd seen others dotting the carriage trails. There was something surreal about these little outposts of human comfort scattered through the wilderness. I thought about those early urban pilgrims, the women venturing from New York City townhouses on a great outdoor adventure, but always constrained, bound by corsets and long skirts and voluminous yards of heavy material encasing them from head to toe. If our paths could cross, what would they think of three half-naked women speeding by on two-wheeled contraptions propelled by means of their own not-inconsiderable power, shouting to one another, scaring the horses? I can only believe that at some hidden place deep beneath their whalebone stays they would envy our freedom and strange pleasures.

••

Where the trail was wide enough, we rode side by side. I took the opportunity to admire my companions and, again, to measure myself against the yardstick of their achievements. Teri was wearing cotton climbing shorts and a bikini top (her T-shirt yanked off and stowed shortly after we started), and I couldn't help but feel a bit awed at the sight of her tanned abdominal muscles, of a kind not often seen outside the pages of fashion or fitness magazines. I reached under my tank top, touched my own stomach and was disappointed to recognize that it even felt fish-belly white. It was clammy, slick with sweat, and, well, maybe a little squishy. Susie rode on my other side, and since she was nearer my own skin tone, I looked to her for some comfort. Our bare arms stretched out so near each other, the first thing I noticed was that where Susie's upper arm displayed the swoops and divots that shout "Biceps!" my own manifested a straight line from shoulder to elbow. In fact, looking at my puny forearms and skinny wrists propped against my handlebars, I was surprised they could even support the weight of my body against them.

The creeping insecurity of self-consciousness was leaking into the exhilaration of the day. But racing over packed dirt, feeling the hum of speed up through my tires and bike frame into my arms and body, I was suddenly over it. Teri and Susie were the strongest women I knew and I was keeping up with them. Under certain circumstances I could even take the lead. In fact, each of us had our strong points. Susie was the bike handler, the best at picking lines through minefields of roots and rocks. I followed close on her rear tire through these sections, following her example. Teri was the boldest, her heavy bike and total lack of fear making her a living missile on downhills. And I was good at climbing. I pulled hard on my bar ends, leaned heavily into my saddle, and enjoyed the view from up front.

●●

Near the top of one long uphill section I slowed almost to coasting. I wiped my face with the back of a gloved hand, drank more water, and tried to take deep, even breaths. First Teri, then Susie, slipped past me and I had to hope a fast sprint downhill would be cooldown enough. I stood first on one pedal, then the other, clicking furiously through gears, trying to catch up.

I was riding a new bike I'd bought just the month before. It had cost three times as much as my previous model, bought entirely with kill fees from commissioned articles that didn't pan out. (I'm not sure what this says about my writing, but I was devoted to the bike.) It made me feel slightly invincible, like a ten-year-old with brand-new sneakers on the first day of summer. It had all the right stuff to make bike riding a joy—it was light, had front shocks, bar ends, clipless pedals, and was a tough shade of matte black.

But my favorite part of the whole machine was the shifting system. It sported grip shifts, which work the same as with a motorcycle—a click of your wrist changes gears. Racing down the side of a steep hill, powering through the gears on my right grip, I couldn't help but think of riding my tricycle as a kid. I'd spend hours riding in circles on the patio, emulating my older brothers who raced motocross, making motorcycle noises as I pretended to twist the molded red sparkle grips of my trike. Suddenly, I felt like doing the same thing again, making speedy acceleration sounds at the top of my lungs as my gears caught and I raced faster forward and down, chasing my friends.

After nearly two hours of riding, with only a few quick breaks near streams and lakes to ensure we wouldn't bonk from heat stroke, we finally reached the highest point on our ride and marked the moment by getting off our bikes. The trail's pinnacle ended in a sharp turn formed by a few massive pillars of rock, so wide and substantial we could walk our bikes out onto them. Standing at the edge of those enormous columns of stone was like hovering free in space. Below us, two unflapping hawks caught an updraft and rose nearly to where we stood. To our right, far below, was Lake Awosting, blue in a patchwork of browns and greens, and to our left were red barns and homes of various hues, extending bright color through the trees.

We stood there for a long time, not talking much, just looking and sweating in the hot sun. We'd been wet so consistently that day that a little more hardly mattered. Besides the constantly replenishing moistness of perspiration, we'd practically bathed at every major body of water we came across. Teri invented the method. Shortly after entering Minnewaska, we'd come to Awosting Falls. Before I'd even known we were stopping, Teri was off her bike with her head underwater. She sat up dripping and wrung out her long, curly hair once, but mostly she let the water spill over her shoulders, soaking her clothes and body. I crouched down and did pretty much the same thing, and so did Susie, though our hair was short and it didn't have quite the same all-over drenching effect. I had to augment with splashes onto my arms, legs, and chest.

Though Awosting Falls is an impressive cascade—three or four stories crashing free fall into a smallish wooded pool so clear that bright blues and greens glow up from the bottom like a Las Vegas fountain at midnight—we'd been alone by the water. No doubt in order to protect its perfect pristine bottom, swimming isn't allowed at the falls. We were its only admirers. People want more than beauty from their landscapes; they want recreation. With bikes, I realized, we had both.

Things were different at Lake Awosting. After a high-speed descent from the overlook, we slowed to a roll at the rock slab that constitutes the beach. There were a number of people, but thanks to the temperature not nearly so many as would normally congregate on an average summer day. If you don't bike into Awosting, the much shorter walking trail to the lake still involves hiking for a good hour, maybe more, straight up. The trail is so steep, that going down it on a bike could be scary in places. You get a decent group at Lake Awosting since it's not easy to bring in coolers, boom boxes, and beach chairs. Though, astonishingly, some people do.

I may not remember what kind of bikes Susie and Teri rode (I think Teri's was pink?), but I recall each of our swimsuits clearly. Susie and I both wore Speedos. Hers was a dark blue one-piece and mine a two-piece triathlon style, also blue. Teri wore a bikini, four triangles and six pieces of string that somehow held everything in place during hours of sweaty climbs and brisk downhills.

Strangely, we didn't go in the water right away, but instead lay back on the warm rock and chatted. We talked about people we knew (and some I didn't), about different runs we might do, about climbing, and about our jobs. It was so bright, the hard sunlight bouncing off the white rock, that it wasn't easy to see each other. We faced the lake rather than each other and watched the white clouds reflected across the water's calm blue surface move slowly along. If not for the green band of forest on the far shore, the lake might have been a seamless continuation of the sky.

After a scanty lunch of fruit and energy bars, we waded into the water. Susie broke off to swim some "laps," as if the exertion of getting to the lake wasn't enough for her, while Teri and I stayed closer to shore, dunking underwater again and again just to enjoy the enveloping pleasure of all that liquid coolness on every part of us. I rolled onto my back and succumbed to the sensation of floating in sky, surrounded on all sides by endless blue. I can't say how long I rested there like that, both time and body suspended, but when I finally rolled over again, reluctantly, Teri and Susie were already lounging onshore.

The ride back was at a blistering pace. We took the steep, straight Awosting trail as fast as our bikes and handling skills would allow. More than once I bounced off rocks and roots and first worried about crashing, then worried about flatting, but not because I was afraid of showing my ignorance if something happened I couldn't fix. I worried because I didn't want to stop, didn't want to slow down. I didn't want to be left behind.

We pulled into Susie's driveway in approximately one quarter the time it had taken to ride out. Throwing our bikes on the grass, we piled into her kitchen where Teri and I stood in front of the open refrigerator while Susie mixed a gallon of ice-cold sports drink for us to chug. We drank standing by the sink and didn't say much.

I hoisted my bike into the back of Teri's truck and we waved good-bye to Susie. As we pulled away, she was hunched over, busy checking a tire. Teri was in a hurry to get going since she still had a job to go out on that evening. The thought floored me. I was thoroughly worked.

I waved once to Teri as she backed out of my driveway, and leaving my bike leaning against the porch, I walked shakily up the front steps, my thighs twitching with involuntary muscle contractions. The house was empty except for the dogs. I headed straight for the refrigerator, where I drank the last half quart of lemon-lime Gatorade and moved a bottle of Sam Adams from the fridge to the freezer.

I took a cool shower and rubbed lotion onto my arms, my thighs, my calves, and felt pleased with my body in a way I hadn't been since before puberty. It worked well; it was strong. What more was there to need or know? I pulled on my clothes without drying off and, like Teri, let the water from my hair drench what I was wearing.

I grabbed the beer and headed out to the porch with the dogs. It was turning toward evening, but the air was still heavy with wet heat. I held the cold bottle against my forehead and watched the rosy light extend upward from the ridge into the darkening sky. I opened the bottle and took a first slow sip, thinking: If this is estrogen therapy, I like it.

NAMING OUR CANYON

• •

Hannah Nyala

"It's a desert oasis, so it isn't going anywhere. We don't have to hurry. Nothing's on fire."

If I said that once, I said it ten times in the first mile, and for every time I mumbled it aloud I must've thought it forty times more, but it didn't change my six-year-old daughter's mind—or the pace at which her feet hit the ground—one bit. Sam, our young search dog, loped along beside her. I trotted to keep up with them.

"I'm not worried about *it* going anywhere, Mommy," Ruth finally said impatiently, illustrating the point with both hands as if explaining a very simple matter to a very simple soul, and never decelerating her feet in the least. "But if we get there sooner, then we can be there longer."

Oh. Now why hadn't I thought of that? So much for my plans for a leisurely weekend backpacking trip with my youngest child. Eight miles round-trip in the southern California desert, Cottonwood Springs to Lost Palms Oasis and back, and three days to do it in; girl talk, woman talk, healing, forgiving, bridging the gap that the last two years of living apart had created between us, finding a way to walk toward a future that still looked rather grim.

Ruth had been home only a little more than a week the morning we set out on our hike, and the anguish of the past two years still weighed heavily on both of us. We were technically safe, yet substantively not, especially in the ways that perhaps matter most. Family violence respects no boundaries; carves out no moats about your existence: Ruth and I were home, but her brother Jon was still living with the man who had battered all three of us, and we had no way to change the situation. So although my daughter and I clung to one another and meant it, there was still a chasm of indescribable dimensions between us as we headed toward Lost Palms that morning. My plan was for the camping trip to bring us back together and give us some reasons for continued hope. Such a good plan it was too. So good it probably deserved the vigorous dusting in the soot of reality my daughter was all poised to give it. She slowed down only twice that morning—once for a chuckwalla and once for a rattlesnake. The rest of the time we hustled toward our destination with all the fervor of a small freight train.

Reaching the hill above the oasis in record time, we headed downward at a fast trot. When we got within an untested stone's throw of its tall trees, Ruthie stopped so abruptly I almost bumped into her. Small rocks skittered out from underneath my hiking boots, and I threw both arms out to the side to keep my balance. Ruth appeared not to notice my difficulties, and I still believe that had to have taken some effort, although she denies it to this day.

"Well, we're here," she said, dropping her small daypack on the ground. "And I'm thirsty."

Perhaps some lingering snittiness about the speed of the journey's first half got stuck in my craw, I don't know, but I replied, one hair shy of testy and with a deadpan face, "Well, technically we aren't really at the oasis till we're under the palms, so maybe we should hurry right on down there before we get a drink."

Ruth looked at me so straight I nearly sneezed. One full second passed, then two, three. Finally she said, "I'm all hurried out. And besides, you said it wasn't going anywhere, Mom." She was chopping my name off, a warning that something about our relationship was problematic at this precise moment.

So I shrugged out of my backpack, planted my bottom on the ground between the soles of my boots, leaned back against the pack, and opened my canteen to take a lengthy, well-deserved swig of water. Something should have warned me, something about the way my daughter looked long and hard in my direction then swept up her pack and replanted her feet on the path as I stretched first one leg, then the other, out in front of me and poured Sam's water onto a piece of plastic set down in a small bowl-shaped hole beside my hip. Something should have looked ominous about the way she set her chin and glared at those treetops and seemed to have forgotten her thirst intact, something, anything. But nothing did. So I was still half lying there, guzzling water and soaking up the warmth of the late summer sun, when Ruth peeled off down the trail hollering out, "Last one to the oasis is a rotten egg!" and Sam took out after her so fast he kicked gravel all over his makeshift bowl and my legs.

Scrambling to my feet, I yelled after them, "Don't let him get in the water!"

Ruth stopped so abruptly Sam ran directly into the backs of her knees. "I know the rules, Mom. I'm not a dunderhead," she shouted, looking intensely at me and putting one hand on one hip. Then, turning on her heel, she fastened the other hand in Sam's collar and called out over her shoulder, "You're still the rotten egg."

In our family, being the rotten egg relegates you to worker-bee status. Ruth had just covered the last two hundred yards of our first four miles faster than I could swallow and stand up. She was now officially Queen of this trip.

Any mother who has unwillingly lost a child lives always beneath the shadow of that terror. Even when the child comes home, fear seeps into your every gesture: You hug her a little too tightly, hold on a little too long, laugh a little too hard at all her jokes, let slide her small moments of defiance, and get way too unnerved when she slips out of sight unexpectedly. Sensory overload. Small wonder that your parental antennae miss the more subtle cues, ones that hint you're being challenged to a race you're about to lose, for instance. Rotten egg—it wasn't simply a metaphor for my rank until sundown. Ruth was finally home and I was catching up. In more ways than one.

When I finally dragged myself into the oasis, Ruth and Sam were perched side by side on a rock, calmly sharing a box of raisins. They paused only long enough for the Daughter Queen to chide and point, "Rotten Egg." Then, same finger trained on herself, she added, "Major Queen."

I curtsied, dropped my pack again, and grumbled something about her having gained the throne through questionable means. Ruth merely raised her right eyebrow dismissively, but as soon as I looked away, she giggled behind her hand. Then she slid down off her quartz monzonite throne, her shepherd-mix gentleman in waiting loping after her, and for the next two hours we all puttered about the oasis.

There's something primeval and lonesome about finding a small pool of murky, insect-strewn water nestled reluctantly at the bottom of a desert canyon that the word "oasis" can never articulate. Although only the most powerful of thirsts could make this liquid appear potable, its presence alone gives the setting a touch of serene authenticity, a feel of deeply rooted connections to those dark, cool streams that flow beneath the parched skin of the ground on which you stand wondering at water's generosity, marveling that it agrees to come to the surface at all, much less stays long enough to collect dead twigs and bugs and algae. Tall swishing grasses grow near the pool's edge, slicing at your legs, and the heavy brush skirts of the fan palms rustle and sway in the contrary breezes that come dueling down the wash, tumbling over themselves and anything else that stands alongside you and the rocks and trees.

I always feel like I'm in church, perched on the very first pew, when I stand at the edge of an oasis. Here God is generous, worth kneeling for and knowing, and is as deeply saddened by cruelty and thoughtlessness as any of the rest of us are—and I know this with a ferocity that surprises even my most determinedly agnostic self. On that day I ventured to voice some of those thoughts aloud and said, "Sometimes I think I can almost feel God here."

Ruth spun around on one toe and glared at me. I waited. Finally my daughter's response came, sheathed in a frown that went from the top of her head to the soles of her feet, "Hmpfh. I'm just about sick of God."

There was no need to ask why, no chance to either. Ruth rushed onward, "Been praying to him a long, long time, and he just about doesn't never do what I ask. Lets Daddy hurt us and stuff. Lets the judge and the cops act ugly to us too. So I think God's a meany, and one day I'm gonna meet him and tell him so, face front."

Face front. Ruth has been heading into life that way from the moment she landed on the planet and urinated on my half-blind, nearly retired obstetrician. There's not a dissembling cell in my daughter's whole body, a trait I've always admired in her, but one I also knew had cost her many harsh punishments over the last two years.

Slowly nodding, I said, "I guess I can see why you'd think that. But, you know, God isn't just a man. God's a woman too, and everything else that we can't even dream up in our heads. It's mostly people that have made God into a man, rewritten books and histories so everyone would forget that God is both female and male."

Ruth tipped her head to one side, considering this, and leaned over to scratch Sam's head. "Nope, he has to be a man, Mom. He's too mean to be a woman." Then, chin set at a stubborn angle, she turned on her heel, Sam in tow, and headed off to look at a small kangaroo rat's nest they'd found nearby.

Breathing in strongly of the heated air, I settled down not far from the sweeping base of a palm tree and lay back on the ground to gaze at the sky, wondering aloud what new tasks my daughter would come up with for her Rotten Egg. Except for a sharp glance or two Ruth ignored me clean, pulled her tiny notebook out of her shirt pocket, and said, "Time for me to get back to work. The botany's waiting."

My response was automatic. "You mean the plants or the subject?"

"The plants."

"That's flora then. If you're talking about the plants—botany's the name of the subject, flora's the word for plants in general. Flora or vegetation maybe."

Ruth's tone dropped immediately to the register for explaining a basic fact to a simpleton. "I know that, Mom. Read those words in my book, but don't like 'em very much. I like botany better."

This was too good an opportunity to pass up. "What's wrong with flora?"

Ruth wrinkled up her nose and paused a moment, then said, "Yeulckk—it sounds like cottage cheese, and that stuff's nasty."

"Oh. But what about vegetation?"

For this one, Ruth had to think awhile. Hand looped through one pack strap, she gazed off into the sky and finally said, "Well, that sounds like vegetables too much, and they're all nasty too. All but spinach." Ruth was into spinach, had requested it two meals a day ever since the first night she'd arrived home. Frank, the park ranger I'd married a few months earlier, had told her that spinach is what made Popeye so strong. She continued, "So botany's better," and, without waiting for me to reply, she spun around on her heel and took off again.

"Botany it is then," I called after her, laughing and wishing once more that kids had the wheel of the lexicon. Ever since I was six myself and learned in first grade that adults had full control of the language I've been resisting that unjust arrangement.

A few yards away, Ruth stopped short, did a little hop step, looked back over her shoulder, and brought me back to the present again with a skip and a question. "So what do you think about the name Felicity, Mom?"

I groaned aloud, Ruth laughed and skipped off with Sam close behind.

This name change business was beginning to sound serious, so I knew I'd have to address it head-on before too long. The very first thing Ruth had announced to Frank and me on her arrival was that she had decided to change her name, "So I'll be trying on some new ones for a while till I can find the one I want best," she said.

When asked why, she answered unhesitatingly, "I want a strong name, a name so nobody will think I'm a wimp and they can beat up on me and stuff."

Hot, flashing streams of pain coursing through me, I flinched visibly, turning partially away so Ruth wouldn't see it, but she was looking at Sam and wouldn't have noticed anyway. She kept right on talking. "It's like you, Mommy. You have a soft name, and you're nice to everybody, kind of sissy, so people beat up on you. I want a hard name so nobody even tries anymore," she'd said, voice toughening as she looked me in the eye and stopped stroking Sam's fur to finish the thought. "And I'm gonna get big and strong and mean as a snake so I can whup on 'em if they do." Almost as an afterthought, she added, "And I'll protect you and Jon too."

I had no words then, no words except another murmured apology for the past two years of her life, and a hug to tell her how dreadfully I'd missed her. Tears standing in her eyes, Ruth locked her arms around my neck almost fiercely and said, "I missed you too, Mommy."

Frank acted instinctively and gave both my daughter and me precisely what we both needed right then. A huge bear hug. Then he took a long stride backward and broke into a wide grin. "Well," he said, "why don't I start teaching you some of the ways that cops like me use to deal with the bad guys?"

Ruth yelped out a cheer so loud that Sam leapt to his feet, while I grinned but excused myself to the bathroom where I could throw up. By the time I'd washed my face and returned to the front room, Ruth was executing her first "takedown" of a grown man and she was beaming. If she is determined to change her name, I decided, so be it.

Still, I'd almost changed my mind since, especially when we rolled through some of her considerations, some of which I was quite sure she'd chosen just to horrify me: Tiffany, Bast, Athena, Deborah, Hera, Alex, Calypso, Frogger, Sam, and now Felicity. Most of these Ruth used only for a few hours, then moved on to another choice. Most were strong women's names, "Grumpy goddesses," Ruth opined, "just like me."

Now, on our weekend alone together, Felicity had come out of the blue, or rather, out of the tiny baby name book that Ruth had worn to a bedraggled mess from paging through it so much. Time for me to speak up. Tonight, I vowed, tonight I'll start telling her Mammaw Ruth's stories again. Then I rolled over on my side and soaked up more of the heated air, confident that Sam was looking out for his new missus.

The loss of anyone we love hurts, but nothing bears any comparison to losing a child. When Ruth and Jon disappeared, I felt as if all that was human about my spirit had been laid open and flayed. The flaying rips open your protective layers, sears your nerve endings, makes your innermost organs shriek mutely. Once flayed, the skin of your soul grows back hesitantly, if at all, and even in the unlikely, miraculous off-chance that the child is returned, as one of mine was, your spirit remains ever-sensitive to touch, instinctively shying away from memories of the event much as a badly burned finger recoils from an open flame. Once flayed, you must teach yourself to trust beyond the loss every breath that comes.

Loss is not a foreign concept among my people, the hardworking, rural Southerners who brought me into the world and nurtured me through my first seventeen years. Wakes and funerals were as common in our county as Sunday dinner on the ground and Saturday night's Grand Ole Opry on the radio, but not near so much fun or with half as much to recommend them. My sister and

I had to wear long dark-colored dresses and socks to these death events even in the summertime, and tight patent-leather shoes, in which we were expected to stand around for what seemed like (and actually were) hours on end. Funerals were things you just did to show respect if you were a Southerner of good breeding, so we both grumbled but we did them anyhow and got good at it.

Then, a few years later, death claimed the woman I loved more than anyone on the planet, besides my father, my horse, and my raccoon, that is—my mother's mother, Mammaw Ruth to me. She was part American Indian and part something else that she point-blank refused to acknowledge or name. On the dreary December morning that she closed her eyes and never opened them again, I finally understood why we had to wear dark clothing to funerals: all other colors tell lies at a time when you really need to be bumping noses with the truth.

Mammaw's death punched a hole in my world, introduced me up close to the whole prolonged business of dying from cancer, broke my heart, nudged me to live better, and gave me my best reason to date for trying to land in heaven when I was done with living. She'd gone ahead of me, that was all, I reasoned, long after we had covered her plain coffin with damp black dirt in the cold drizzle from a sky I was absolutely certain would never again welcome back the sun. I truly believed the world had stopped right along with Mammaw's heart, and I numbly plodded through the day of her funeral feeling very little, noticing nothing at all but those cascading red roses that I despised with every cell of my body. It took years to make sense of her "passing," years to make peace with the loss, years to believe that she was gone from sight and touch, from smell and hearing, but otherwise not gone at all.

To this day I yearn for the feel of her strong, gnarled hand on my shoulder or head, the sound of her deep, rasping voice telling me her Indian stories, the sight of her big old belly jiggling with laughter underneath her flour-spattered apron. But I remain unflayed. It's the child for which you've cared and loved and lived and breathed that lays you open to that. So I lay on the desert floor, one child home and doing botany, one still gone, and carried myself back over the decades to where my head was cradled in Mammaw's lap while she shelled butter beans in a big tin dishpan just above my face and told me story after story of how her people came to be in this world.

Ear pressed to the ground for no better reason than that I'm always curious to see how close someone has to be before I can feel them approaching, I listened to my daughter come marching toward me. She was scuffing her feet, which meant she was getting sleepy too. Sure enough, in a couple minutes, she plopped down on the ground beside me, and Sam stretched out between us. Now our trip was fully under way.

Deserts demand siestas. Even a live wire like Ruthie can't evade the convincing urge for a nap that reaches out invisibly and gives you a warm hug whenever the sun starts its long slide toward the western horizon. Ruth, Sam, and I were curled up near the shady edge of a big boulder, sleeping intermittently, watching the palm fronds lift and wave slightly in the wind.

Something inarticulate occurs when you rest outside in a desert. All that's petty drops away from you, like a dry old skin sheds off a rattler, leaving her shiny and young again, if momentarily sightless and off balance. You blink the sleep out of your eyes to see with an unexpected clarity and suck in great tingling gulps of newly unearthed oxygen. I always stretch—long, gradual, semi-deliberate lengthenings of each muscle group—and feel keenly the sand grains biting into my back or arm or leg. It's a powerful way of coming to terms with the parts of my existence that defy explanation, this ability to lie steady, noiselessly, on a tiny bit of ground in a land that many people shun and fear as too harsh, too forbidding to even walk in or visit, much less sit down or sleep on. Sometimes, if I'm still enough, spiders use me as an anchoring point for a new web addition: that's what was happening that day.

Grateful the Queen wasn't awake to squawk the poor creature into retreat, I lay on my side and watched the small fearless fellow throw himself off the limb of his creosote bush home and touch down lightly on my thigh. Now a thin gossamer strand connected me to the bush, and as I watched, the spider headed back up the filigreed cable.

All of a sudden, Ruth screamed and sat straight up, and I sat up right along with her. Lord only know where the hapless spider landed.

"What is it?" I asked, alarmed when it became apparent Ruth wasn't protesting the spider's presence—as near as I could tell, she appeared not even to have seen him. She kept screaming, flailing with her hands, hitting me, Sam, herself even. Grabbing her arms, I shook her sharply, and as quickly as she'd started the outburst, Ruth stopped, her body went limp beneath my hands, and she looked into my eyes and finally saw me.

I waited. Slowly, with difficulty, she opened her mouth and whispered, with tears shimmering in her eyes and pouring down her cheeks, "He's hurting Jon again."

Instinctively, I sucked air into my lungs and looked into the abyss of my daughter's eyes, seeing there a pain that mirrored my own. I knew then that she, too, had felt this lash, that the screaming agony of losing a child is not, indeed, the worst thing that can happen to a person: Ruth had lost her brother, and she grieved for him every bit as deeply as I, his mother, ever could. We sat in shuddering silence. Sam stepped from one of us to the other, settling his head first on Ruth's shoulder, then on mine, and finally he lay down so his body would be touching both of us simultaneously.

I had no heart to lie, to tell my daughter the kind of senseless soothing words both she and I knew were false anyway. There was a very good chance Ruth was right, that even as we snoozed and reconnected in the desert, her brother was being beaten for some tiny, real or imagined infraction of his father's rules. Maybe he hadn't folded his T-shirts neatly enough this morning. Or had left a spot on one of the glasses. Or had been beat up by a bully at school.

For long, untimed moments, we sat hunched in the sand, silent and sober, both lost in our own worlds of longing and sadness. After a while I took Ruth's hand in mine and said what I always did: "One day Jon will come home to us, Ruthie. One day he will."

Ruth listened gravely, then looked up at me and replied, "Yeah." After a long while she added, "And then he'll be a thorn back in my neck again, huh Mommy? Always bossing me around, stuff like that."

"Undoubtedly," I said, smiling at her, grateful that of all the maternal traits she could have wound up with, Ruth had somehow gotten the best one, an unflinching pragmatism.

Ruth responded by squeezing my hands and then scrambling to her feet. "He's a knucklehead, but I guess he can't help it. He *is* just a boy," she said, as if that explained everything. She stalked off. "Now I need to get back to the botany."

I rolled over and listened to her footsteps retreating, and closed my eyes against the tears that kept rushing in, and listened hard for my son. Before long, I was dozing again.

Minutes later I stretched awkwardly and opened my eyes, feeling heartsore and stiff, but refreshed and ready to get up—and looked directly into Ruth's and Sam's faces. Ruth broke eye contact only long enough to check her watch, and I could tell from her expression that that wasn't the first time she'd done that lately.

"You've slept twelve whole minutes, Mom!" she grouched. "Don't you think it's time we found us a place to camp tonight?"

Next thing I knew we'd shrugged back into our packs and were heading down toward Victory Palms. We scrambled up the canyon's southwest side so we could find a good campsite, far enough away from the oasis that our presence wouldn't frighten any animals who depended on it. Ruth was hiking now like a seasoned pro. No longer on a trail she knew, no longer in a hurry, she even slowed down and stopped periodically to look behind her so she'd have some idea where we'd come from if we got lost. I'd taught her that again the very day she came home.

"So you track people, Mommy. Do you ever get lost?" she asked, referring to the fact that I had taken up search-and-rescue tracking for the National Park Service in her absence.

"Well, I'm sort of paid not to," I replied.

"But do you?" Ruth asked again and stopped walking entirely, waiting for my answer. It didn't take a functioning genius to know she would be deciding whether or not to continue following me based on what my answer was.

Luckily, I could reassure her with the truth and say, "No," because Ruth can spot a lie at thirty paces, and there were only twelve between us.

"Well, good," she said, and I heard her feet start hitting the ground behind me again.

We soon found a spacious level area with plenty of small boulders scattered thoughtfully about its edges for camp furniture. By the time I'd fired up our tiny Primus stove, Ruth had set our "table," with Sam sitting patiently beside her. Long before the sun was anywhere near gone, we had finished supper and were playing hopscotch. I lost, but that was only because the Queen chose to exercise her right to order me to put both feet down on the ground NOW! just as I was closing in on a well-deserved win. Sam received his first-place trophy from the royal highness herself, then came over to console me as I grumbled some more about monarchical privilege.

"What about the name Bast?" Ruth asked suddenly, referring to an Egyptian cat goddess she'd recently met in a library book. Striking a goddess pose that was remarkable only for the height at which she managed to hold her nose in the air, Ruth said imperiously, "I am Bast, goddess of all I see. And some that I can't."

So we were back to Bast. It was time for me to speak up, so finally I said what I'd been thinking all week. "But tell me true now, why do you want to change your name? I think it's one of the prettiest names I ever heard—one of the strongest, too. I wish it were mine even."

"Good then. You can have it."

"I'm not going to take my own daughter's name, mizzle head. You didn't answer my question. Ruth's a strong name—why do you want to change it?"

"Don't like it."

"Why not?"

"It's not pretty, it's plain. Just Ruth. I want a pretty name, a song name maybe," she said and burst into a tuneless "Help me Rhonda, help help me, Rhonda." "Maybe Rhonda would work. Now you see? Isn't that better than Ruth, just Ruth?"

Before I even had a chance to answer, she hurried on, "I want a big name, too. Not a weak name like yours, Mommy. People are mean to you, and you just let 'em be. But I'm gonna be different. Strong. Punch 'em in the nose maybe."

For the second time in ten days I saw myself through my daughter's eyes. She really meant it. She had a weakling for a mom. A wimp. No matter that I avoid most confrontations largely because I feel they're a waste of spirit and spit. No matter, either, that my reasons for refusing to fight back against her father on my own behalf were based on my strict adherence to principles of non-violence. My way had worked reasonably well, too, during the six years of our marriage anyway, because he beat only me, not the children. But Ruth saw the inside of her world, had to reckon with the blunt fact of living with her father without me there to absorb his anger, and from that angle, in her eyes and my own as well, I must surely come up wanting.

No matter that I had done my dead-level best to find Jon and Ruth and bring them home, but wound up out of money, very ill, and hopelessly outmaneuvered by a justice system that would rather have children beaten regularly than intervene between a biological father and his offspring. No matter any of the reasons or justifications. Ruth sincerely believed she had a wimp for a mom. Gritting my teeth to hold back the vomit, I told myself sternly that this attitude would serve her well in the long run: if she kept up this tack, held onto these insights, no man would ever beat her again. Meantime, I had a job to do, and it was close enough to bedtime to begin it.

"Ruthie, I feel like there's a long, wide canyon running between us, a canyon like Lost Palms, only bigger and deeper, and it doesn't have a name. It's like we were holding hands and walking along together until the day your father kidnapped you two years ago, and then all of a sudden you were over there on one side and I was over here. Do you know what I mean?"

Ruth nodded, then looked directly at me and said, "He told us you didn't love us no more."

"What did you think about that?"

"I hollered at him that it was a lie, but he beated me bad for it, Mommy, hitted me with the broom."

"I can't fix that hurt, Ruth. I can't even give the canyon between us a name, but I can tell you that you were telling the truth. I have always loved you and your brother, from before either one of you was ever born, loved you more than anything else in the world. Nothing has ever changed that; nothing ever will. Do you believe me?"

She nodded slightly. We'd already had a couple versions of this conversation by then, so Ruth had a fair idea of how hard I'd tried to bring her and her brother home again.

"So I am very sorry that I seem weak to you now, but someday I hope you'll see that I have pretty good reasons for being the way I am. Doesn't make it perfect, but it works for me, and we'll sit down and talk about all that when you're ready. But now we need to get back to this name change thing. Do you remember all the stories I told you when you were little?" I asked.

"Umhm," Ruth nodded, smiling widely. She did remember very well. She'd asked for one backrub and four stories a night every night since she'd been home, so I knew she remembered them.

"Remember I told you once those were my grandmother's stories?"

"Yes."

"Well, I think it's time you learned a little more about her."

Ruth shuffled her bottom around and trained her shining eyes on me.

'Mammaw's name was Ruth Haney. She was an Indian, born in Mississippi in 1899 and lived there all her life, so you can guess she had to be one of the toughest, meanest women on the planet just to survive—"

"Daddy said she was just a stupid old sharecropper without no schooling," Ruth interjected. "And he said you sound stupid when you call her Mammaw, too. Says that's a name only uneducated people use."

"Well, I think words like 'Mammaw' are proud and important, and you need to use them as often as you can, because English needs all the help it can get. It gets downright sick in the head if some of us don't break its rules regularly, know what I mean?"

"Yes ma'am," Ruth said. She'd heard my views on the language before.

"That means you say 'ain't' and 'Mammaw' and 'Lawsy Mercy!' and whatever else you can think of that sounds like the normal people around you, and you just flat-out ignore your schoolteachers when they tell you any different. If you get in trouble, I'll back you up on it, all right?"

"All-righty, I b'lieve I got it, lawsy mercy I do!" Ruth was now so happy she was pounding her fists with excitement on the ground, ready to jump into the conversation with both feet.

"Good."

"I'm Indian too, Mommy—got a card that says so."

"Yep, you're a registered Potowatomi—that's a little bit different from Mammaw Ruth, and she didn't ever get a card, but that's just one more thing you two have in common. Now what you really need to know is that four months before you were born, I knew you would be a girl—don't know how I knew it, I just did. Knew deep inside that you'd be an ornery, knotheaded little girl just like I was when I was your age, exactly like Mammaw Ruth was all her life. And I made up my mind right then that you would be named after her." Pausing a moment to let that sink in, I went on, "Now, I'm not about to sit here and tell you you can't change your name. You can, if that's what you really want to do and you ever find one that you'll stick with for more than three hours." Ruth grinned and tossed her head around defiantly. I was right. She had been gig-ging me with some of those choices.

I continued, "But if you do decide to change it, I want you to do it knowing full well that the name you're choosing to set aside is the finest, most special name of the finest, most special woman who ever set a foot on this planet. Ruth Haney. And it just so happens that she was the strongest person I've ever known, too. Tough as nails, with a backbone of steel and a heart to match, she used to say. Didn't let anybody walk on her or hers either. So if you throw away her name, you'll be throwing away all that strength, and you'll have to get some more on your own. So you need to think about this name change really hard before you go on with it, okay?"

Finally I sat quiet, spent from my outburst. Ruth nodded, crawled over and sat beside me, and said, "Mommy, I really think it's about bedtime, don't you?"

"Sure," I said, looking up at the four o'clock sun shining down on our heads. "Sounds fine by me."

Whooping and hollering, Ruth rushed over to her cotton mat and waited almost patiently for me to sit down and pull off my shoes, then lie back on my own mat beside her. Sam looked at us as if we were crazy, and he stood there at our feet for a couple minutes, but when we didn't get up, he finally stretched out between us, chin on his paws but still ready in case we came to our senses and got up to finish out the day.

"Storytime!" Ruth chortled, and I groaned and rolled over on my back, pretending to be really sleepy. "Come on, Mommy—tell me a story, one of Mammaw Ruth's stories."

I groaned again, and Ruth upped the ante. "I'll let you off being the Rotten Egg."

"As well you should, too. You cheated anyhow," I said, covering my eyes so I wouldn't glimpse my daughter's face and inadvertently laugh.

"Okay, then tell me six stories in a row, and I'll promise not to cheat you anymore. Anymore this week."

I lost the round exactly as I'd planned to. Within minutes we were deeply immersed in Mammaw Ruth's stories. By the time the moon stood full over us, my throat was so hoarse I could hardly talk, and Ruth finally fell fast asleep in the crook of my arm. These are the hours that help you forget the flaying, help you remember the hope. Desert nights don't simply promise healing; they practice it. They give you a chance to sink inside the regenerative contours of the earth itself, to step outside the demanding rush of society, conversation, automobiles, human noise, and smells, and your own expectations of yourself, and simply breathe yourself back from the brink.

The next morning I woke with the sun and made a cup of tea. An hour later I poked my sleepy daughter and said, "Well, get up, lazy head, the day's half gone."

Ruth groaned, and I reminded her that she'd wanted us to find a boulder to practice climbing on today.

Ignoring that entirely, she sat up, hair tousled, eyes still half shut, and said, "I dreamed about Jon last night, Mommy."

"You did?" I said, voice determinedly flat.

"He was here too, right here with us, listening to Mammaw's stories. We were sitting right there on the ground telling them, and you know what happened?!" Ruth's eyes were now wide as saucers, not a trace of sleepiness left in them. I didn't even have time to shake my head in response to her question before she burst onward.

"Mammaw Ruth come walking up, from right over down by Victory Palms! She walked right on up here big as day, wearing that big white apron and walking beside her big old white bulldog, and you know what she did? She sat herself right by me and said to that dog, 'Now Baby Boy, you behave yourself and don't beat up on their scrawny little yellow city mutt'—that's what she said about Samson," Ruth gulped and paused for air, but rushed on again. "And then she hiked her dress up over one knee and said, 'I hear yall been tellin my stories over here,' and we said 'Yes'm' real quiet, just like so. She nodded her head again and said, 'Well, yall got some of the p'ticulars wrong, and I'm here to set you younguns straight.' That's what she said, Mommy!" Ruth was talking so fast she could hardly sit still. Finally she gave up trying, scrambled to her feet, and rushed over to where I was sitting.

"Sure sounds like Mammaw Ruth to me," I replied. "What else did she say?"

"Oh, well, she just told us every single one of her stories again and fixed the p'ticulars you missed—you didn't miss anything important though, don't worry."

Ruth was starting to settle down slightly, so I offered her some granola for breakfast, which she gobbled down so quickly I thought she might be sick, suggested as much, and was rewarded with a grin but nothing else in the way of compliance. Then I broached the topic of rock climbing again, and Ruth thought a long while about it. Thought so long I had our bed mats and sheeting rolled and stowed away in my pack before she answered.

"It's like this, Mommy," she finally said, "there's rocks we can climb near home."

"Yes. So what are you saying?"

"I want to go home. Maybe we'll get a message from Jon."

"But this was supposed to be a weekend camping trip," I

protested. "Three days to spend just us together in the desert, fig- uring out a way to cross that no-name canyon between us and such."

"Well, we can do that at home easy as here, can't we?" Ruth asked, so reasonably I couldn't argue.

"Sure we can, I guess," I said. She was right, after all. One patch of desert isn't necessarily any more special than the next. Given that we lived in Park Service housing, with only a radio for com- munication, it took a while for phone messages to get to us any- how. And even longer for us to drive to a phone where we could respond. If Jon was trying to reach us, we'd never know it way out here. For the first time ever, I regretted living inside a national park.

Ruth knew full well what I was thinking. She followed it up with a sensible suggestion. "Well then, let's go home."

"Home it is," I agreed. We hoisted our packs and headed back for the canyon. Reaching it, Ruth took the lead and kept us all mov- ing at a fast clip for about four miles straight. When we passed Mastodon Peak, a small chunky rock hill near Cottonwood Springs, about half a mile from home, Ruth finally stopped and said, "Whew! I'm really thirsty!"

"Too thirsty to walk and drink at the same time anymore?" I asked skeptically, since that's what she'd had us doing the whole way.

"Yep."

"I don't know. Sounds like a trap to me. Hey Sam!" I called. "What do you think? Is she angling to be Queen again here or what?"

Ruth giggled and spilled water down her shirt, and Sam wagged his tail happily, ready to go or stay. He didn't appear to care much which right then.

"Come sit over here by me, Mommy," Ruth said. "It's not a trick, promise, needle in the eye and stuff."

I charily set my pack down and eased over to her, while Ruth basked in the glory of yesterday's successful subterfuge. But she didn't move.

When I got properly seated beside her, she reached over and took my hand and said, "That no-name canyon? The one you talked about?"

I nodded and she went on. "I was thinking we should give it a name."

"Oh," I said, caught entirely off guard. Ruth held onto my hand firmly with one of hers, and patted it absentmindedly with the other. "I was thinking we could call it Knucklehead Palms, Mommy. What do you think?"

I said the first thing that came to mind. "But it doesn't have any palms in it."

Ruth looked taken aback momentarily, but she recovered quickly and said, "It does now. Mammaw Ruth planted a couple last night when she come by."

"Oh. Okay then, I like that name, I guess. Fits pretty well."

But Ruth wasn't finished. "And Mommy, I was thinking maybe it'd be better if I don't change my name for now. I can wait till I get older, I think."

"All right," I said. Then warily I added, "How old?"

"Oh, maybe when I'm ten or so. Ten's real old, huh?"

I was just about to agree with her, to say ten was practically ancient, in the range of Methuselah at least, just about to let her know I was glad she'd decided to wait and how proud I was of her and how happy I was she was home, just verging on saying that whole set of lovely, mushy things . . . when Ruth leapt to her feet, snatched up her pack, and yelled back over her shoulder, "Last one to Cottonwood Springs is a Rotten Egg!"

Her ponytail and Sam's tail rounded the first bend simultaneously ten seconds later, about the time I made it to my feet, and I could hear Ruth laughing proudly, the sound staccato-like and retreating as her feet pounded the ground.

Clearly I still had some catching up to do. I shouldered my pack and galloped off down the path toward home, heading up the far side of Knucklehead Canyon at last.

THE SOLO JOURNEY, REVISED

••

Lea Aschkenas

Mount Chirripo, Costa Rica's highest peak, is a rock tower looming nearly 13,000 feet above a landscape of surreal contrasts. Dusty trails crisscross and dead-end into clear blue lakes that appear like mirages in the middle of a desert. The seventeen miles of uphill terrain alternate between mosquito-infested jungle and fire-blackened forest. In the early morning, jackrabbits chase each other through parched brush, and at sunset the sky echoes with the cries of wild boars.

Mount Chirripo splits the country in two. If you reach the top before the afternoon fog rolls in, you can see the Pacific on one side and the Caribbean on the other. In the evening, the temperature drops below freezing and icicles decorate the roof of the plywood hikers cabin. But in the afternoon the sun is so intense that half an hour without protection can leave your skin bubbling.

The ranger station requires cabin reservations a month in advance, and although the national park surrounding the mountain is only sixty miles from the San Jose bus terminal, it takes a full day of travel on potholed dirt roads to get there.

It makes no sense to head off to Mount Chirripo unprepared. But there are times when life makes little sense, when a relationship ends, when your return flight home is fast approaching and you realize you haven't had that life-altering revelation you left the States in search of. Like the view from Mount Chirripo, your life splits in two directions: here and there. And you understand with sudden clarity that you must leave, prepared or not.

This is where I found myself the year after I graduated college. My six-month reporting internship in the capital of San Jose had ended, and I decided to seek direction through spontaneity. When I retell this story, I feel I should be detailing a solo journey, the type you read about in those revelatory travel memoirs in which the heroine ventures off into the woods and encounters only herself and discovers, to her surprise, that this is enough. But this is not my story. Rather, I decide to go with a friend because I am feeling alone and not up to a solitary vision quest and, most important, because my friend's willingness to leave on a day's notice makes me feel that what I am doing is perfectly normal.

This illusion begins to dissolve as I start packing and realize that I am missing most of the supplies necessary for a trek of this intensity. At the beginning of the month, someone stole my muddy hiking boots from the welcome mat of my house in the city. So on the morning that Eleanor and I leave San Jose, I am sporting a worn pair of Nikes, barely adequate for running on city streets. A few weeks before my decision to hike Mount Chirripo, I lent my roommate my large hiking pack. By the time I realize I need it for myself, she is already two weeks into her monthlong camping trip in the Guatemalan rain forests. Somehow I manage to stuff my sleeping bag, a wool sweater, two pairs of shorts, long underwear, and a camera into a small book bag for the five-day hike up Mount Chirripo. I am pretty proud of myself until Eleanor points out that I have forgotten about food and water.

She mentions this with a tinge of sarcasm in her voice, and I wonder whether she is still upset about our morning trip to the grocery store. We had argued over what food to bring as we walked through the aisles. I wanted bare subsistence and light backpacks. Eleanor wanted variety at any price. While she turned her back to grab something off the shelf, I replaced her guava juice with water, her trail mix with instant oatmeal, her cup of noodles with bread. But when we got to the checkout, I discovered that Eleanor had caught on and, among other luxury foods, our shopping cart contained trail mix and mangoes, and my oatmeal was nowhere to be found. Finally we settled on a compromise: trail mix, peanut butter and jelly, bananas, and two loaves of bread; bottled water for me and tropical juice boxes for Eleanor.

Eleanor had a large hiking pack, so she agreed to take the food and drinks. I told her we could take turns carrying the packs, but she refused. Although she would admit to no ulterior motive, I think she feared for the future of her dried papaya.

Eleanor and I had met at our internship two months earlier. We bonded over long dinners and philosophical discussions in Casa Yemaya, a woman's hostel where we both stayed while looking for housing in San Jose. We assumed that because we got along well at work and were compatible hostel mates, we would also make good traveling partners. But then, we had never spent twenty-four hours a day together in the wilderness, in the beautiful yet brutal simplicity of nature that distills even the best of friendships into their most organic and sometimes basest components.

••

Although we arrive at the San Jose bus terminal early in the morning, there are no seats left on the bus to San Gerardo, the alpine village that is the starting point for the trek to Mount Chirripo.

"We should have bought tickets yesterday," Eleanor says, but as I reluctantly nod my head, a small, stick-thin man standing at the front of the bus motions for us to come up anyway.

"*Ustedes caben,*" he says. You'll fit.

He walks ahead of us to the back of the bus, waving his arms wildly in front of him so that everyone clears to either side. He takes our packs and sticks them in a corner, atop a sack of mangoes, and then heads up front to recruit more people.

I spend the daylong ride attempting to balance myself between a bicycle wheel and the mango sack. The window closest to me will not shut, and when the afternoon showers begin, the rainwater soaking my clothes becomes indistinguishable from the sweat coating my body. The rumble of the unpaved road drowns out conversation, so Eleanor and I entertain ourselves by watching the thin man play jack-in-the-box with the other passengers. He taps their heads and then ducks behind the backs of their seats while the passengers turn around, laughing in confusion as the exhaustion of the long ride gives way to giddiness.

The absurdity of this situation is almost too much for me, and I laugh so hard I am nearly crying. Eleanor reaches into her backpack and pulls out a mini-pack of Kleenex with the Safeway price tag still on it and offers me a piece. Eleanor is prepared for everything. Whereas I had come to Costa Rica in much the same way that I decided to go to Chirripo, Eleanor had prepared for her trip to Costa Rica in the same methodical way she tried to plan our mountain trip. She had come to Costa Rica after two years of planning and saving up money. When I told her about Chirripo, Eleanor wanted to buy bus tickets that day. She wanted to call a hotel in San Gerardo and make a reservation immediately. She had attempted to fill our grocery bags with enough food for a good month's worth of gourmet meals in the outback.

After the jack-in-the-box man finishes his show, Eleanor neatly repacks her Kleenex and, turning to me with a look of untimely seriousness on her face, tells me that she's thinking of going home.

"What do you mean?" I ask. "You still have four months left at *The Central American News.*"

"But I can't do it anymore," she says. "I like writing but I hate journalism. I'm not interested in politics. I don't like writing on deadline. I never even buy the newspaper at home. I read novels."

"Well, what will you do then?" I ask.

"I don't know," she says. "I was hoping to sort things out while we're away."

I try to think of a response, but nothing comes. I had counted on Eleanor to be the grounded one on this trip. I had never considered the possibility that, in her eagerness to join me, maybe she, too, was running away from something.

"Look, the rains have stopped," Eleanor says pointing to the horizon where the sun is setting a fluorescent orange against the midnight blue. I nod my head, thankful for the distraction.

The sun is all gone by the time the bus pulls up to the Mount Chirripo ranger station. The jack-in-the-box man walks over to Eleanor and me and, waving his index finger in a shushing motion across his lip, says, *"Oye, el noche empieza."* Listen, the night is beginning. Salsa music and moon fill the spaces of sky between the waterfall-fronted mountains of San Gerardo.

When we step off the bus, the thin man tells us, "You've come at the best time. The rainy season could end tomorrow." He waves his hands out in front as though to hypnotize the sky into obedience. "If you think it's crowded now, wait until the dry season. That's when everyone comes here. You don't want that—tourists, crowds. *Como Disneylandia*," he says. He wrinkles his forehead in distaste, and his mustache follows like a marionette limb.

"My name's Marcos," he says, reaching out to shake our hands. "Do you like to salsa?"

"Yes, but I'm not very good," Eleanor says.

I tell him I like to try, and he points to the right side of the dirt road, next to a wobbly wood plank bridge, like the ones kids dare each other to run across in the playground. A cluster of turquoise-painted wooden cabins glow almost eerily in the last moments of sunlight. The front cabin is set aside from the others and has a sign advertising Pilsen, Costa Rica's national beer, nailed above the door. The building seems to be swaying, almost moving in rhythm to the salsa music that emanates from inside it.

"Those are mine," Marcos says. "Cabina y Bar El Bosque. We just opened last month, and we're the cheapest *cabinas* here. Come with me. My sister-in-law Rosa will make you dinner. We have hot showers, and across the bridge I will show you hot springs where you can bathe."

Eleanor and I exchange furtive glances, but as I look around to examine our other options—I nod at Eleanor. We follow Marcos down a path in between the shadows of the pine trees, to our *cabina*.

Inside we change into clean clothes, and Eleanor jabbers on happily about a panoramic disposable camera she's bought to capture the views from the peak of Mount Chirripo. But I am having trouble focusing. I feel somehow betrayed by Eleanor's earlier disclosure of her uncertainty about her present situation.

After dinner, Marcos offers to give us a guided hike to the hot springs, suggesting that the minerals there will heal us and prepare us for tomorrow. He carries a flashlight behind his back like a child switching fists in a game of "guess which hand." We follow cautiously as the mud pulls at our shoes.

"Ah, tranquillity," Marcos says when we arrive at the hot springs. He sits down on a rock and pulls his shirt off.

I nudge Eleanor but she nudges me back. "Thank you for bringing us here," I say. "But we don't have bathing suits."

"*Tranquilo. No pasa nada,*" he says, the Costa Rican version of "Don't worry. Be happy."

A howler monkey cries out in the distance, and as I'm trying to figure out how to respond, a beat passes, and then another, and then the silence informs on its own.

Marcos pulls on his shirt and stands up. "Okay," he says. "I will wait in the woods so you can undress. I will wait with the flashlight, and you just call out 'Marcos' when you're ready."

Eleanor and I sit silently in the hot springs. The heat is numbing, and steam rises and hovers above my exposed shoulders like a protective layer from the cool evening air. I can no longer see the path we took to get here. It seems to have evaporated into an invisible quicksand hole once we entered the springs. Although I know I could not find my way back on my own, I feel certain the image of this place will remain imprinted in my memory. It's a strange phenomenon that the places that always remain most vividly in my mind after my travels are the places that are unrecorded elsewhere, that no guidebook has found. Maybe it is because I know I can encounter them nowhere other than in my mind that I remember and cling to them with such intensity. Maybe it is because I do not understand how my mind works and do not trust it to record forever the memories I want to keep for the sake of nostalgia. Too often it has failed me, recording the moments of regret and confusion with a clear lens, allowing the times of courage and forgiveness to blur over and fade into the background.

••

The next morning, we start out on our hike. Once we leave the rush of the rapids behind, we enter silence broken only by the soft pat of our feet as we walk on a forest floor carpeted by spongy leaves freshly soaked from the previous day's storm. For the first half hour, Eleanor and I walk together, passing from the open green valley that surrounds Cabinas y Bar el Bosque into a dense jungle filled with so many mosquitoes that we have to use tree branches to swat the space in front of us in order to see.

After our first water stop, time somehow speeds up for me while it slows down for Eleanor. I have been so immersed in my fly swatting that when I turn around I realize that the space between Eleanor and me, originally only a few dozen feet, has increased to an unknown distance. I can no longer see her so I wait for nearly twenty minutes before she catches up. This happens once more, at our next allotted meeting place at the end of the jungle trail.

"Here," Eleanor says, handing me a water bottle. "Take it and go ahead. We should just meet up at the cabins."

I listen for any hint of anger in her voice, but there is none. So I accept the water bottle, carrying it in my right hand and sometimes swinging it in front of my face as part of the fly swatting routine since there is no room for it in my book bag. I pass very few other hikers. When I do encounter others along the way, unsure of what language we have in common, our conversations consist of brief head nods and smiles, reassurances that all is safe where we've hiked in from.

The next stretch of trail, which completes the fourteen miles to the cabins, is a stark contrast to the previous jungle trail. In 1992 a fire burned through this upper path, and today the remaining trees stand like leafless charcoal stretches. The wildlife seems to have retreated to the lusher first half of the trail, and the silence along this part of the trail is interrupted only by my own footsteps. At every few turns I look back, expecting to see Eleanor around the corner, but she is never there, and I wonder if maybe I should just wait for her. Sitting on a rock between scurrying lizards, I have a brief philosophical moment. If your pace is different from someone else's, do you save time by making frequent stops along the way, or is it better to just head off on your own and wait for a large chunk of time for her to catch up in the end? Isn't the middle of the hike and the feeling of ecstasy that comes at its conclusion all part of the same journey? I realize that before this trip, I have always hiked on my own or with friends who have walked at my same pace. And I'm having trouble reconciling my desire to do this hike the way I want to do it with my sense that I should be willing to make the compromises necessary to sharing a wilderness trip with someone else. I contemplate this for a good fifteen minutes, but there is still no sign of Eleanor, and, remembering that she suggested I continue on in the first place, I stand up and head off on my solitary trek, passing through this desert silence in a time warp.

A small creek appears like an oasis, and I lean over to splash water onto the rough saltiness of my face. But I forget that I have my book bag on and, light as it is, it propels me forward too quickly and I do a face dive into the water. I think about scratching some warning message in the sand of the trail for Eleanor, warning her not to do as I did, but then I realize that given Eleanor's orderliness, the chances of her forgetting to remove her backpack are slim. Still, since I am the one who has deserted her and gone ahead, I feel an obligation to consider possible calamities Eleanor may encounter. And at the same time, I feel resentful about this self-imposed sense of duty. I want to just be here on my own mentally. During this time, I want to be figuring out what I will do with my life when I return to the States next week.

But in this moment, there is only this desert scape, and I continue on through jutting black tree limbs and sun-bleached logs with red flowers growing out of the dead rot. Lizards scurry in figure eights between my feet and I feel dizzy as if in a time warp, the landscape at each step a déjà vu of the past several miles. My stomach is beginning to ache with hunger, and the sun is slowly descending beneath a stretch of prickly, icicle-shaped rock formations in the distance. I hear a voice echoing to my left, and when I turn I'm relieved to see the Costa Rican flag waving next to two cabins, the shelters where we'll stay before making the next day's journey to the peak.

Inside one of the cabins there are two rooms—a bedroom with queen-size bunk beds and a kitchen where several Frenchmen are drinking red wine while they make tomato sauce with fresh tomatoes they carried up from San Gerardo. In the bedroom, a couple I remember from Marcos's *cabinas* is sipping hot chocolate. My stomach lets out a small growl of regret. What had I been trying to prove with my sparse food supplies? Why hadn't I planned this trip earlier so I would have had my hiking pack and room to carry food on my own? Why had I put Eleanor's cup of noodles back on the grocery store shelf?

The couple, who introduce themselves as Spencer and Amanda, offer me a cup of hot chocolate and ask where Eleanor is.

"We should look for her," Spencer says. "You know the boars come out at night."

Waving a flashlight back and forth between the naked trees of the burnt forest, we take turns calling out Eleanor's name. It echoes through the landscape, but there is no response.

"Maybe you should go over there," Spencer says, illuminating a cliff with his flashlight. "Maybe she'll hear you better there."

I call out again, and this time when the barren land returns my own name to me, it is followed by a crashing sound.

Spencer and I hobble down the cliff, and Eleanor is lying in the dirt below, surprisingly close to us.

"Something ran in front of me," she says. "And then you called out and I slipped somehow."

Spencer takes her backpack, and I help her dust off her leg.

"I'm okay," she says to me as we're walking back. "The worst thing was thinking that after all this hiking we've got nothing to eat for dinner but peanut butter sandwiches and bananas."

"We'll just go to bed early," I tell her. "So we can sleep through our hunger. We'll be okay in the morning. It's only three miles to the peak from the cabins."

Distance in the desert can be deceptive. When there are no landmarks, no trees, and there is no change in scenery, how do you determine how far you've gone? When even the ground, a soft orange sand, returns no evidence of your passing but instead swallows up your footsteps into its ripples, how can you be certain that you have not just been treading in place, moving deeper into a quicksand of stagnation?

For the first mile of the hike the next morning, Eleanor and I trudge along slowly together. Except for water, a loaf of bread, and the jar of peanut butter that I am carrying, we have left our baggage in the cabin, but somehow the lighter load does not make the going any faster. I feel as if my body is still defrosting from the night before when I realized that I didn't have the right type of sleeping gear for below-zero temperatures. I spent much of the night trying to curl myself as small as possible and enviously watching Eleanor sleep uninterrupted in her multiple layers and ski hat and gloves, her body wrapped in the trash bag she'd brought as a rain cover for her backpack.

An hour into the hike, at the point where the peak of Mount

Chirripo comes into view, the sun comes out, and the desolate land, motionless except for the occasional tumbleweed, bakes like a clay oven. My skin loses its frosty feel and, once again, the distance between Eleanor and me grows. This time I hand her the water bottle and we decide to meet up for lunch on the peak.

Once you reach the base to the final summit of Mount Chirripo, the only way to tackle it is by crawling, by holding onto its jagged edges as long as you can, until your hands feel near ripping. Halfway up, hunger hits me in the form of a swirling dizziness, and the only way I can push on is by telling myself that I can collapse at the top, lay on a flat surface and eat, since I have the food this time. Something about the air rejuvenates me when I reach the top. The oceans on either side are obscured by fog, but the mixture of cool cloud cover and sunlight stabilizes me, and I think that maybe I can put off eating until Eleanor arrives.

There is only one other person here, one of the Frenchmen whom I'd seen cooking dinner the night before. He seems to be meditating, so I sit on the other edge of the peak and look out. I close my eyes and lay back, feeling the sun cast a kaleidoscope through the clouds onto my eyelids.

I wake to the sound of Eleanor's voice telling me how red I look.

"I'm still thawing out from last night," I tell her.

"It looks like sunburn," she says. "Did you bring sunscreen?"

I shake my head. Another detail overlooked. Eleanor hands me her sunscreen, and we sit in silence, admiring this land that seems to stretch into infinity.

I make myself a peanut butter sandwich for lunch and Eleanor makes two.

"I have to," she says. "I realized climbing up here that I'm afraid of heights, and I need all my strength to get back down. I'll just eat less for dinner."

Eleanor makes it down with much coaxing and, exhausted, we both walk together all the way back to the cabin. We arrive a few hours before sunset, and I decide to try out the shower. It's a gray metal cubicle between the bedroom and the kitchen, and I learn, too late to just jump out, that the pipes release only ice-cold sheets of water.

When I get out, I tie my hair up to prevent its chilliness from touching me, and I join Eleanor in the bedroom. The scene is much the same as it was the night before. The French people are sitting on the floor eating an aromatic meal over a picnic blanket encircled by flickering candles and a fresh, steaming loaf of bread. Spencer and Amanda, on the bed above ours, are splitting a brimming pot of garlicky black beans and rice. And a woman who is already decked out in a ski parka and scarf is opening a bottle of wine.

Eleanor is sitting on our bed, staring blankly into her backpack.

"What's wrong?" I ask her.

She opens her backpack for me. There are only two slices of bread left, some peanut butter, and an unopened jar of strawberry jelly.

"How'd that happen?" I ask.

"I don't know," she says, and simultaneously our stomachs roar.

"Well, you did have two sandwiches for lunch," I say, incredulous that I am being this petty and unable to stop myself.

"Lea," she says, a look of shock on her face, "I can't not eat tonight. As it is, we don't have breakfast, and we have that fourteen-mile hike back."

"What do you want to do?"

"I want to eat the sandwich."

"What? The whole sandwich?"

"Yes, I've got the bigger pack. I need more energy."

"But you ate two sandwiches. I want this one and . . ."

I feel something tapping my shoulder and look up to see Amanda's arm extended from the bed above, a pot of half-eaten rice and beans in her hand. Several other hikers are looking on in disbelief.

"Here," Amanda says, climbing down from her bed and placing the pot between Eleanor and me. "A peace offering."

We eat so fast, we burn not only our tongues, but our lips too. We eat in silence and go to sleep soon after, angry and embarrassed.

We both wake at sunrise the next morning.

"You look really burnt," Eleanor says. "Your eyelids are swollen."

My face does hurt, but I am having trouble distinguishing frostbite from sunburn. The stinging sensation has been with me since yesterday morning, and I am already dreading the long, painful hike back to Marcos's *cabinas*.

"You should put some of this on," Eleanor says, handing me a tube with aloe that cools my face like a brief splash from last night's shower.

In return, I offer Eleanor the jar of peanut butter.

"We can make a sandwich and split it," I tell her, and, in what I take to be a gesture of acceptance and friendly restraint, Eleanor does not bring up last night's argument and instead nods her head silently, a subtle smile forming on her lips.

I feel weak on the trek down, slow even, but still lose Eleanor less than an hour into the dusty desert descent. Maybe she was right that her heavier pack added something to her time. Or maybe she was still limping on her injured leg two days after her fall. I once again contemplate waiting, but decide against it, knowing that my stopping will not help Eleanor to go any faster, and that hiking together might irritate us both, breaking the spell of our silent reconciliation.

I march through the familiar terrain robotically, trying to keep my sunburned appendages from banging against each other. In the jungle, I am too tired to swat at the flies, and I look down so that there is less eyeball surface area for them to glue themselves to.

Stiff and sweaty, I arrive in San Gerardo around two in the afternoon, and after the best lukewarm shower of my life, I settle in on the bed and read a book while I wait for Eleanor. I read one chapter and then another and another, and then there is no more. And my stomach begins to growl. And once again, the sun is about to set.

I walk down to the kitchen where Marcos is still entertaining the locals. He is balancing a plate of *gallo pinto,* fried rice and beans, on his head as I walk in.

"Oh, it is our lost one," he says, pointing to me. "I was just saying that it was getting dark and I was getting worried. Where is your friend?"

"I don't know," I say. "I've been waiting in the room for her, but now I'm getting hungry."

"Well sit down and eat," Marcos says, removing the plate from his head. "I have been keeping this warm for you. Regain your energy, and then we'll go looking for your friend."

As I am wolfing down my last black bean, a bolt of thunder strikes in the distance. And then the rains, as if in competition with the surrounding waterfalls, come pouring down, pelting against the tin roof of the kitchen.

"Let's go," Marcos says, standing abruptly. He goes into a back room and returns with a large umbrella for the two of us, and we head into the darkness, calling out to Eleanor. Tonight there are no echoes and no resounding crashes, and we walk past the waterfall and into the mosquito terrain for what seems like quite a distance before there is a response to our frantic calls of "Eleanor."

This time the answer comes in the form of a moan. Partially sheltered beneath the leaves of a large palm, Eleanor is lying collapsed in the mud.

"I thought I might die," she says softly, deliberately, almost matter-of-factly when she sees us.

Marcos takes her backpack. I help Eleanor to her feet, and we position ourselves on either side of her for support. Together the three of us stumble back to the *cabinas,* a silent, limping, muddy monster emerging from the undergrowth of the jungle.

Over her dinner, Eleanor sniffles and tells Marcos of our misguided adventures, of her fall on the way to the cabin, of her discovered fear of heights on the way up Mount Chirripo, of the slimy root she slipped on, landing her beneath the palm on the hike down.

Marcos sits calmly, smiling knowingly as Eleanor relates her list of misfortunes.

"I've seen it before," he says. "People come here looking for the real outdoor experience, but no one has told them that this usually comes in the form of a bruise."

After we pack up, Marcos walks us to the bus and hands us a present of bananas for the ride back.

"Have you decided what you are going to do about *The Central American News?*" I ask Eleanor when we get on the bus.

"I'm going to stay in Costa Rica," she says. "I don't want to leave yet. It's only been two months, but I'm going to quit the internship. I'll just find another job. I think going on this hike was really good for me."

"Are you serious? After everything that happened?"

"Well, I had a lot of time to think while I was alone," she says.

"When I was alone, I was worrying if you were okay," I say.

"Hey, you're the one who invited me," Eleanor says laughing.

I feel relieved that it's okay. That at least our friendship is still intact even if I have not found any of the clarity I'd been seeking during this hike.

Eleanor dozes off for the rest of the bus ride, and at the bus terminal in San Jose, as night is setting in, we make plans to get together early in the week before my flight back to the States.

I fall asleep almost immediately when I arrive home. Most of my belongings, including my alarm clock, are packed, and when I wake, fully alert in the dark, I can't figure out what time it is. I am still on camping time, when you go to sleep at sunset achy and sore and wake, refreshed, at sunrise. I wander the house looking for a clock and then decide to go out and watch the sun rise, a solitary awakening, the type I would have had during the hike had I gone on my own. I cross the street and sit in a swing seat in the children's playground that faces east. I push off the ground and, trying to enter into a meditative state, breathe in on each backward sway and exhale on each forward one. I listen to the swing set creak in a lulling rhythm while I wait out the humid darkness of the predawn, anticipating the moment when the shadows will recede into a familiar landscape. Waiting for the sun to rise.

DRIVING

••

Mary Morris

Because I have a baby who will not sleep and a car, two things I haven't had before, I begin to drive. I put Kate in her car seat and drive up to Los Angeles. We go to Watts Tower, to the Getty Museum. We drive over to Venice and walk the boardwalk.

We stroll past the souvlaki shops, tie-dye stores. An aging hippie sells ankle bracelets she is making on the spot. A man carves a mermaid out of wet sand as people drop coins in his cup. On Muscle Beach men with huge pectorals and bulging biceps are pumping iron inside a chain-link cage. Brown-skinned girls in bikinis sculpt their thighs while roller skaters, dog walkers, and joggers amble by, the sharp sounds of their exhales sounding like someone blowing on reeds. A tiny black man with stumps for legs and only one arm whizzes past us on a skateboard. Pausing just ahead he does a little dance on his stumps, shaking his butt. Not far from him a man with a sign that reads SINGLE FATHER: PLEASE HELP US sings with his daughter. She is perhaps five and has barrettes all through her hair. They put their faces together as she croons, "I Shot the Sheriff." I hand Kate a dollar, which she lets fall in their hat.

Then I drive up the coast highway and we stop on Malibu Beach. A film crew is shooting on the beach; surfers ride the waves. I park along the side of the road and take Kate for a walk, her feet wading in the sea. We race up and down the shore, toss pebbles into the sea. Suddenly there is a rustling in the waves. Something dark appears. I look up and there is a pair of dolphins, not far from shore. So close I feel as if I could reach out and touch them. I pick Kate up, pointing. "Dolphins," I say, racing with her into the surf. The water soaks my jeans. Kate throws her head back and laughs as the dolphins frolic near us for what seems like a long time.

We lie in the sun to dry off, then stop for a burger somewhere, and Kate devours French fries soaked in ketchup. We share an ice cream cone, then I find a supermarket nearby where I stock up on what we need. There's a sale on diapers and I buy a box of forty-eight. It is dusk when we get on the 405, heading home. Kate likes the movement of the car, the wind on her face. Soon she is asleep and she sleeps all the way home.

It is late when I get home, and Stan has parked in my space. I have discussed this with him before. I've asked him to please leave me a space to pull in behind the house. He's got his pickup, and his wife has her car, and he doesn't seem to see what the problem is. Now he's done it again, and I have to park down the block.

I have too many things to carry—groceries, the cooler, Kate. I take Kate up to the house first, slip her gently into her crib. Then race back to the car for the groceries. Before I even reach the car, I can hear her screaming.

• •

I grow weary of the 405 with all its traffic, so one Sunday I venture east. It is a road I haven't traveled before, Interstate 15, heading to Nevada. I pass Barstow, drive through Summit. I know I should turn around, but I keep driving. Where am I going? I ask myself, but I don't turn around.

Pink alkali flats take on shapes. As I drive, I think I see caravans, a village, herds gathering on the hills. A golden lake shimmers before me, but as I approach, it turns to sand. Except for the passing truckers and ghost towns where men sit on porches, sipping beer, tattoos snaking up their arms, this desert is all mirages. I drive for hours, my forearm resting on the open window, the sun searing my skin.

In the rearview mirror I see Kate, asleep in her car seat. A rim of sweat on her brow, a thin coating of dust on her cheeks as if she is another apparition. If I stop, she'll wake up, so I keep going, further into the Mojave, stretching like a blanket of yellow, red, lavender in all directions.

The last gas station was maybe an hour, two hours back. Maybe it was open, maybe it wasn't. The gas gauge hovers just above the red danger zone. I should have stopped back there, but I didn't. I don't know how to change a tire or what to do if the radiator overheats. Who I'll flag down for gas.

All I have with me is a jug of warm water, and the CB radio my brother sent me when I moved west—the CB sits in the trunk, never installed. A voice tells me that none of this is a good idea, but still I keep moving. The radio plays "Mamas, Don't Let Your Babies Grow Up to Be Cowboys," but I lose the station in mid-song. Kate starts to fuss and I'm feeling the heat as well. Just across the Nevada border I pull over at a marriage chapel. This one is called "The Hitching Post." I like its name. It has a soda machine and a gas pump and offers weddings twenty-four hours a day, no blood test. The A-frame of polyurethaned logs has a front porch where Kate and I sit after I fill the tank, where I pay the boy who seems to have appeared out of nowhere.

On the porch is an outdoor altar with a bald eagle, a faux mountain backdrop, a dream catcher. Kate winces as I wipe her face with a Wash 'n Dri. I give her a bottle of juice and put coins in the soda machine that sells Dr Pepper bottles. I buy a bottle and then peer inside the building where there is a small church altar and Jesus, bleeding, a mournful look on his face, on the Cross.

Soon the first couple arrives. They wear cowboy boots and Stetsons, jeans. Their witness is drunk and staggers along behind them. He invites us to join them. It's the third time they're getting married to each other, the witness says. JUST MARRIED AGAIN is painted on the side of their van. Kate and I move in closer as they knock on the door of a shack, waking the minister. The minister comes to the door, rubbing his eyes, and a few moments later he emerges carrying a Bible and wearing a white shirt. Money is exchanged, and the couple opts for the outdoor Native American altar.

The ceremony is quick. If you blink, you've missed it. Kate reaches into the green Tupperware container, hurling rice a little too soon, hitting the minister in the eye. I sip my Dr Pepper as the newlyweds give a holler, then stagger back to their car, kicking up dust with their heels. They wave and honk as they head west, full of dreams.

When I don't know what to do with myself, I drive. It becomes what I do on the weekends. I can't seem to stop. One Sunday I am driving on the road from the Sierra Nevada toward Yosemite. I have been on the road for five, maybe six hours, passing through one ghost town after another. Kate is in her car seat, but she has been fussing for a while and I know I should stop. I did stop an hour or so back in Victorville at the Roy Rogers and Dale Evans Museum, where we gazed at the real Trigger, stuffed, behind glass, in all his former splendor, and the real Bullet. At the one hundred stuffed animals Roy killed with his own hands, his collection of wristwatches, the shrines to the couple's three dead children. Then we drove on.

I must be crazy, I tell myself, but I keep going, further and further into the Mojave. We pause for a late breakfast at the Olicante Ranchhouse. The ranch house has dead birds mounted everywhere—even on the tables—dead flies, Jesus pictures, red curtains, several mooseheads, and German tourists. Taxidermists must do well in this neck of the woods. We order the cowboy breakfast—steak and eggs. Kate smears scrambled eggs into her mouth. After breakfast I clean her up and start to drive. We make it past Red Mountain, a boomtown founded in 1837, now in ruins. Old cars line the dusty streets in junk heaps; gray laundry hangs on a line.

I had got up that morning and started to drive. I longed for home, for Manhattan and its gritty streets, for people walking at their frenzied, thoughtless pace. I couldn't take another weekend alone with no plans, no one to do anything with. No one I could count on. So once again I drive east on the Vegas road. Maybe I'll just keep driving and go home, but then I turn, thinking I'll make it to Yosemite and back in a weekend.

In dried-up desert towns I play the slots, order malted milks, and then I can't stand it anymore, and I phone R. from phone booths that stand in the middle of dusty fields. I talk into his machine for as long as he talks into mine. I tell him I want to get married. I tell him I love him and we should try again.

In the middle of one of these calls he picks up. "I'm so glad to hear from you," he says. His voice is warm, lilting, like coming home, and I know I cannot pull myself away. From those phone booths in the middle of desert towns, he tells me to be patient, to wait. He has finances to settle, his sons need to grow. He'll be ready to accept more responsibility soon. Sometimes I ask for money. Not much, a little help, but he always sighs. He has so many demands on him. If I could just not add to them. He'll see me at Valentine's. I'll fly there. "I'm short of cash," I tell him.

"Put it on 'Sign and Travel,'" he says.

In one of those towns just after I make such a phone call, a man with tattoos up and down his arms and beer bottles piled on his front porch offers to buy Kate. He says, "If you want, I'll trade this dog for her." He points to a mangy, mongrel dog. The man laughs, taking a swig of his beer. He says he'll call it an even trade.

I get in the car and drive away with her as fast as I can, dust rising in my wake. I get back on the main road, heading back towards the 15 and drive straight until I come to a house where the outside is shingled in street signs. There is a parking lot filled with old tires and toy trucks, all painted in primary colors. A sign reads VIS-ITORS WELCOME, so I stop.

Signs cover the front of the house. LIVE BOMBING AREA, STOP IN THE NAME OF LOVE, WOMEN ENTER AT YOUR OWN RISK. It doesn't seem too inviting, but Kate is squirming, fidgeting in her car seat. I could give her a little rest, maybe get a cold drink, assuming this is some kind of a bar. A man comes out to greet us. "Please," he says. He wears a BEAM ME UP, JESUS T-shirt and introduces himself as David.

"What is this place?" I ask him, as I peer into the patio covered by an old tarp, supported by a red-and-white striped barber-shop pole.

"It's my house," he says, inviting us in. We sit in the patio where giant coconuts and painted pinecones hang from cacti. The patio is strung with Christmas lights and utility lights ("borrowed" from the old railroad that used to run through here). David flips a switch and the Christmas lights come on; the railroad lights begin blinking on and off. Water begins to flow from overhead pipes into an open barrel of water where plastic animals swim. Streamers of flip-tops that dangle from the top of the tarp and are decorated with old eyelash curlers and pots and pans, including bedpans, are suddenly illumined in this strobe light and water show.

Kate rearranges the plastic animals in the water, moves all kinds of pipes and wiring around, bangs Christmas ornaments together so that they wave in the breeze, chases a litter of kittens, as I sip cold root beer. David brings me a plate of rice and beans that tastes delicious. He says he's lived here for years now on a pension. "I collect things," he tells me, as if I hadn't noticed. "I guess that's what drove my wife away."

We stay for an hour or so. I tell him I need to get back, and he offers us the guest room. He points skyward and I see five single bed mattresses on his roof. "Up there?" I ask him.

I think how lovely it would be to sleep on his roof under the stars. Then I think that I don't know this man and that Kate could slip off the roof while I slept, so I decline.

"You know what you should call this place?" I tell him, as we head to our car. "You should call it the desert mirage."

"I'll think about that," he says, pressing something into my hand. I glance down and see a nugget of solid gold.

As we are leaving David says, "Here, I got something for the kid." He hands her a small plastic statue of a friar. When he presses on the friar's head, the figure's pants fall down and water squirts out of his penis. David starts to laugh and so does Kate, but

I tuck the nugget into my pocket, grab Kate by the hand, and say to David, "I think we better get going."

We head out into the parking lot, and I can still hear him laughing.

I've come to dread the rain. Whenever I get in the car, I check the weather report. I can't bear it when my windshield wiper flips and I can't see. But the weather promises to be nice today as I'm driving north up the coast. I'm not sure how far I'll get. Maybe Big Sur. Maybe not quite so far, though in fact we get pretty close.

Kate and I stop somewhere along the coast highway. There are paths we can hike through. Horses graze in the valley below, along the seaside. We linger there most of the day. I give Kate a picnic of cut-up banana and peanut butter, which she licks off my fingers. When I let my eyes gaze at the sea, she wades into a patch of poison oak. I give a holler, scooping her up, and she slips her hand on to my breast. Later I will develop a most annoying case of poison oak, but Kate, it seems, is immune.

It is dusk as we head back south. We drive for a long time, but then near San Luis Obispo I see storm clouds overhead. Already a light rain is beginning to fall, and I know I don't want to drive in it. "Let's spend the night somewhere," I tell her. The Madonna Inn is nearby, so I see if we can get a room for the night. A few rooms are available. They are expensive, but I've got the credit card. It's a splurge I know I shouldn't make, but I can't resist. We check out the Safari Room, which is done in faux tiger and zebra skin, the Tack Room (too many whips), the Old World Room (too fancy), the Crystal Room (too breakable). Each of these rooms is what Mrs. Madonna sees in her dreams. She has a vision, then she executes it. I can't help but think of Forest Lawn and much of what I've seen since I've come to California; this is a place of dreamers. We peer into the Cave Man Room, which is too primitive for a mother and daughter, and in the end I opt for the Old Mill.

The Old Mill Room has a miniature working mill wheel above the bed and water churning around the upper moldings of the room. Kate and I have a bite in the dining room, decorated in neo-bordello with gilded grapes dangling from the fixtures, then we play with the mill until bedtime. Finally we drift to sleep. I am exhausted and asleep as soon as my head hits the pillow, but in the middle of the night something jars me. I wake to the room brightly lit, the mill churning, water splashing on to the bed. Gleefully Kate dips her hands in and out of the water, drenching me.

DEAD RECKONING

· ·

Kathleen Dean Moore

Dead reckoning is navigation by deductive logic. When you can't see the stars, when you don't have any landmarks, you can sometimes figure out where you are by knowing where you started, how long you have traveled, and what course you have taken. Columbus used dead reckoning to find the Caribbean four times, measuring his speed with rhyming chants, an hourglass, and the beating of his pulse—but that doesn't mean it's easy. With dead reckoning, everything depends on knowing where you were in the first place—the *last well-determined position,* the Coast Guard says. Then you need to know what direction you are going in, which is not always clear at sea where wind and currents pull a boat off course. You need to know how fast you are moving, and this is tricky too; there is *speed*—how fast you are going relative to the water, and then there is *speed made good*—speed relative to the earth. When everything is moving under you, the difference between what you intend and what you actually accomplish can be the width of a shoal.

"So can you point through the window and tell me where to start?" I had asked the clerk in the marine supply store in Prince Rupert harbor. He gave me a long look, but he closed the cash register drawer, walked to the window, and pointed. "Right there, between those two islands. See the channel?" In fact, there were a dozen islands and as many channels. "No," I said. Reading his face, I could see questions that reflected the doubt in my own mind. How would we ever find that one distant, perfect island we had picked out on the map? *Deductive* reckoning, *ded.* reckoning, *dead* reckoning.

I lean against my truck, trying to remember everything I once knew about finding my way. My daughter is bending over brand-new marine charts spread on the hood. She is penciling in vectors, drawing a careful zigzag line through passages between scattered islands. The harbor smells of gasoline and fish-packing plants—salty seaweed drying on the rocks, gutted fish, bubbly lines of gills and pale sausagy intestines drifting on the tide. These are smells I know and love. I do not want to leave this harbor. Erin looks up from the charts. "We can do this," she says.

I sit down on the dock. This is so complicated. We were supposed to have launched on inland water and motored up passages between islands entirely protected from the sea. Among inland passages, weather would be no threat, and finding our way along fjords would be as easy as walking a ditch. But the back road to the launch site is closed for bridge repairs, and here we are in a deep-sea port instead—the northernmost harbor on the British Columbia coast—plotting an alternative course that will take us miles into the Pacific before we eventually arrive at the inland passages. We can buoy-hop for some of the time, but we're going to have to do most of this by dead reckoning because we don't know these waters and we have no way to tell one island from another. There will be reefs in the lee of the islands, but worse yet, on the long reach when we round the headland at the entrance, it's wide open ocean. I'm not convinced this is wise.

"We'll take our time loading up—launching the boat, stowing gear, getting gas," Erin says. "We'll take a run around the harbor. We'll stop and reconsider before each step, and both of us have veto power. Either one of us says *no*, that's it." I bristle at being the one who needs to be reassured—that's a mother's job, not her daughter's—and really, my preference would be to sit down and cry for a little while here and think this over. But I'll go along with her plan: If we're going to make this run, I want to make it in daylight, and if we're not, I want time to find a camp.

Erin backs the trailer down the ramp. Honestly, this might be the dumbest thing I've ever done. Loosening the winch, I unhook the boat and take hold of the bowline. Erin backs in until the trailer is completely submerged and bubbles rise from the taillights; then she hits the brakes. Slowly the boat floats backward off the trailer. I know better than to take a twenty-foot fiberglass skiff into the open sea. I tie the boat to the dock. Erin accelerates up the ramp and parks the rig in the parking lot. She walks back down the ramp, carrying four food buckets at once. If conditions are perfect, this'll be easy, but with wind or fog? I carry down the chart case and an extra anchor. Erin jumps in the boat and starts to stow gear in the cabin. This is the north Pacific, not some little pond. I hand in two kayaks and Erin straps each one to the rail. My daughter is twenty-four years old. She helped drive this boat in the inland passages last summer. She is experienced and skilled. I hand her the kayak paddles. But she's the same person who sideswiped the ticket booth at the drive-in movie when she was sixteen, and never even knew it. Looking around to be sure we haven't forgotten anything, I lock the truck and carry down the dry bags. I cast off the lines and lower myself into the boat. I guess the worst that could happen is we would drown. Erin looks at me, sits a minute on my silence, waits another minute. Then she whoops and turns the key.

That engine never starts on the first crank. Two hundred horse-power sit there looking stupid. A couple of fishermen lean out the window of their seiner and whistle. But on the second crank, the engine churns and spits and Erin is backing away from the dock and we are actually going to do this.

It's four o'clock in the afternoon. The sky is overcast. It's 60 degrees Fahrenheit. The wind is ten knots from the northwest. There is a line of fog at the western horizon. With the Prince Rupert channel marker bearing 145 degrees, distant 200 yards, we take departure. The bay is black, littered with piles of seaweed and fish offal, amputated logs, scuffed and yellow, and buoys marking crab pots. "Flotsam and jetsam," I shout over the thrum of the engine, but Erin laughs. "You've got it wrong," she shouts. "Jetsam is what you throw overboard to keep from sinking. Flotsam is what floats on the water after you've sunk." I stand in the stern in a cloud of gasoline fumes, absorbing the vocabulary lesson.

Gradually, the harbor goes hazy and the mountains fade from green to gray. When I look ahead, all I see is a confusion of islands and leads that might be passages or might be bays. Behind us, our wake parts the sea neatly into two curling walls, and between the walls, the prop churns the water into a wide white path clearly drawn on the sea. I remember teaching our children to read maps this way—not asking them to plot a trip on the map, but showing them how to mark where we have been. Two little kids strapped in the backseat of the car, leaning over a triple-A map, holding yellow markers in their fists.

Erin has the charts spread out, all ordered near to far. Between shoals in the passage, she picks a way carefully from buoy to buoy, turning to meet the wakes of incoming trawlers. Then we're crossing a bay, motoring slowly to the southwest, squinting into light that gleams on the swell, hiding deadheads and drift nets. We pass a small Tlingit village, then steer around the bedded reefs of an island and move into another channel. A seiner churns by, trailing diesel fumes and a strand of seagulls.

I have put myself in charge of spotting buoys, the markers that connect the charts to the sea. This is the issue—right here. Deductive logic is fine, as far as it goes. But you can't figure everything out in advance, plotting your course on the chart and then chugging along the pencil line as if it were the real thing. Now and then, you have to get a fix, you have to learn where you are, not by where you expect to be, but by what your senses tell you, what you learn from the shape of the horizon. With binoculars, I pick up a pillar buoy dead ahead.

But now we motor from the protection of the island into the open sea. The bow rises on each swell and drops with a thud into each trough, lifting a screen of water that smacks on the windshield. Erin eases off the throttle, slowing the boat, raising my pulse, skidding up the back of each wave, then sliding the boat off the side and plowing through the slick. She must know I'm afraid, because she points to a peak vague on the horizon and then to a headland marked on the chart. "Do you see the mountain there?" she asks. "When we're to the lee of that, we're in protected water. After that, it's a cruise."

When did this happen, that Erin knows how to do this better than I do? How did it happen that she has coaxed me into making this trip, when last I looked I was giving her M&M's to bribe her up a mountain trail? Why should she be unafraid, when my heart is scrabbling against my ribs like a rat in a box?

Erin's paying attention now, ducking her head to look through the swath of windshield where a wiper is swatting back and forth. Here in the entrance to the sound, the tide is running out and the swells are rolling in. Where the forces collide, they throw the wreckage of waves high into the air and the boat dives and pivots in the chop. Erin heads into the biggest waves, altering course to keep water from washing in on her stern, doing her best to keep slop from throwing the boat around and smacking over the bow. I think I see the blow of a whale, but it might be sea spray, and I don't look twice. I don't want to lose concentration on the task at hand, even though it's Erin who is handling the boat and my main responsibility now is to be afraid for both of us.

I've just about decided we are rooted to this pitching place, when suddenly the seas are calm and I'm surprised by the smell of hemlock and the warmth of the breeze. I can see individual trees on what had been a vaguely dark shore, and there are gulls on the rocks, pecking at their feet. I take off my raincoat and stow it in the cabin.

Erin looks around carefully, then turns again to the charts. Now that we're inland, the challenge is to find the way through a maze of channels and inlets to the particular island where we will meet the others tomorrow. Dusk is coming on, but it will be a long dusk in the northern summer. Slowly now, no hurry. If it gets dark we'll find an anchorage and lay over for the night. I feel the calm of the water working on me, settling in my shoulders, and the weepy exhaustion and exultation that come with relief.

It's slack low tide, so the passage is a trough eighteen feet below the shoreline, and fallen trees jut over the water, trailing ropes of bullwhip kelp. We motor past islands perched high on basalt pedestals topped with hemlocks and huckleberries. Through a narrow passage we motor slowly, the engine noise echoing off granite cliffs, then around a hidden reef and into an inlet and on north.

The darker it gets, the more closely I scan the shore for moorages, studying the charts to learn if the bottom is rock or sand. I climb onto the bow and coil the anchor line. We see eagles now, immense dark birds with heads and tails that disappear against the cloud cover: eagles sitting on snags, or on rocks, or soaring under overhanging trees.

As we round a narrow point, there, on high ground, is a black wolf. Erin cuts the engine and we coast to a stop, silence catching up to us and sliding over our heads. The wolf abruptly turns and disappears. We stare at the place it had been—the matted grass, the algae-slicked rock, a pocket of sand. Then I climb down from the bow while Erin comes out of the cockpit. We meet in a long hug, as if we were meeting in an airport, as if we had each come from very far away to get to this place.

Venus has risen over the mountains by the time we reach the island we're seeking. It's too dark to set up camp. At tomorrow's high tide, we'll off-load the gear onto the island and pitch the tent on the point. Frank and Jonathan will fly in, and we'll put out the crab traps and fish for salmon and kayak in and out of the bays. But for tonight, we'll have to sleep on board.

Erin brings the boat slowly into the narrow passage where we will set anchor. When the boat is in just the right place, I drop the bow anchor and signal Erin to put the boat in reverse. As she backs the boat away, I pay out line until I feel the anchor grab. A hard tug to be sure it's set, and I let the boat pull out the rest of the line. "That's it," I call, and Erin turns off the engine. She walks to the stern and lowers the second anchor. While I pull in rope at the bow, she pays out the stern line until the boat is midway between the two anchors. Erin tests the anchor's set, throws out more line, and wraps the rope around a cleat. I secure the forward anchor, leaving enough slack in the lines that the rising tide can't lift the boat and carry it away with its anchors hanging below like fishing lures; but not so much slack that currents can wash the boat onto rocks and damage the propeller.

Setting an anchor is something I know how to do. The slow-motion dance, the forward and back of it, the partnership, the soft movement of the tides past a boat at rest, the sureness of our hold on the earth—there's a joy in this, a kind of homemaking, and when the anchors are set and the engine is finally quiet, silence settles around us like snow and a sea lion exhales somewhere in the passage. We tie our kayaks to long lines and push them overboard. Shoving aside the rest of the gear, we spread sleeping bags on the deck and slide in.

Evening. Bedtime. It's a time for mothers to be mothers, this time when darkness gathers. Stories. A song maybe. Plans. An extra blanket, tucked under a child's feet. How many times have I put Erin to bed on the edge of water? Tonight, the salt-drenched air, the smell of hemlocks hanging over the bay, the trace of gasoline, the silence, make me think of so many other nights.

When Erin was young, we camped at the edge of rivers. When the sun dropped low enough to throw the canyon into shadow, I knelt in the doorway of the tent, holding Erin's fuzzy, floppy-footed pajamas. With one hand on each of my shoulders for balance, she put one foot in, then the other, then I zipped her up, one long zipper from her foot to her neck. Then I would pick her up and carry her to the edge of the water. She sat on my lap, or her father's, and we watched nighthawks hunting insects low over the water, swooping skyward until they almost stalled, then dropping to the river, making a sound like a bullfrog. Later, stars cast flicking lights on currents and riffles, and bats came out to hunt. We counted bats together and when we got to ten, it was time for Erin and her brother to go to bed, tucked in a tent with the breeze blowing through.

I thought then that I knew what would happen next. That Erin would grow up and I would grow older. I thought I had it figured—time moves in a linear progression, and no matter how much Erin changed, I would always be twenty-seven years older and that much wiser. But experience sometimes tells against the theories, and the course line is not always the course made good. It never occurred to me that when my daughter grew to be an adult, we would be grown-ups together; that she would learn things I couldn't teach, would love the water even more than I do. It never occurred to me that someday I would look to her to keep me safe. It's okay, I guess. It's good. I'm just surprised is all.

Much later, I'm awakened by a splash and the hollow knock of a kayak against the hull of the boat. Erin's sleeping bag is empty. The night is black and moonless, the sky dazzling with stars. Wrapping my sweater around my shoulders, I stand up to look over the rail. I can see Erin's silhouette in a kayak, paddling slowly around the star-littered bay. Every time she dips a paddle, glittering light streams off the blade and swirls in the eddy of her stroke. Her bow-line glistens where it touches water. Pushing through biolumines-cent plankton and jellyfish, the kayak leaves a luminous path in its wake, a hundred galaxies blinking on and off, a million stars sparkling like the Milky Way. My daughter, kayaking on the night sky, so many miles from port.

How astonishing to find ourselves in this place. I know where we began. I know how long we have been going in this direction. Maybe what I didn't understand was how quickly we have traveled.

POLAR STAR

••

Susan Fox Rogers

Kate and I turned off I-70 toward Basalt, south into the Rocky Mountains. Our destination was a trailhead where we would begin an eight-day backcountry ski trip. As at the beginning of every other trip we'd taken for the past four years, our legs were tight with anticipation, and a cold sweat lay just beneath our first layers of polypro. Like the waves of adrenaline flowing through my system, our talk stopped and started. We focused on the weather, *yes, it's definitely going to storm*, speculated on trail conditions, *what are the chances that the trail will be broken?* and recited a list of all the things we could not forget: avalanche shovels, maps, compass, handwarmers, the code to the locks on the huts.

As always, Kate was our navigator and I drove. Overstuffed with packs, ski boots, and the large bag of bagels that sat still warm on the backseat, our small rental car appeared to shrink as we moved into a landscape that became steeper and whiter.

"There's a lot of snow here," Kate stated the obvious.

For a long moment she was quiet, her concentration on directions and the weather too keen. This was a bad sign. If Kate was worried, I should worry. The car slid on the thin layer of freshly plowed snow.

We had made our reservations for the huts in the heat of a New York summer. Craving snow and momentarily forgetting that these mountains are four times bigger than anything near our homes, we had become overenthusiastic. That now translated to a desire to buy twelve more bagels, add another sweater to my pack, and call my mother.

"What did we have in mind?" I tried to laugh to ease the tension. Leaning over the steering wheel, I peered up through the windshield, seeking the summit of the surrounding peaks.

Suddenly this all felt huge: the mountains too big, the snow too deep, the trip too long. We both knew it could be the last for a while—in the horizon lurked grad school, maybe even babies. But I didn't like the *this is it!* sensation because I equated these trips with my friendship with Kate. Without them, there was no us.

Kate and I met over ten years ago through the rock-climbing community in New Paltz, New York, where our paths circled one another but never intersected. She was popular: long wavy red-brown hair, skinny, an excellent climber, runner, skier—just the type of girl that my experience in high school taught me was not my friend. I didn't care about my clothes or nails enough. I didn't want the boys to like me. What I couldn't see from a distance was that Kate didn't care either.

The first time Kate invited me to go skiing, yes was my immediate response. But within seconds I was worrying: I'd never skied with a pack on my back. I didn't own backcountry skis. "You'll do fine," Kate was confident. But bigger than the physical worries, I wondered at spending a week with a woman I hardly knew. There were only two obvious outcomes: either we'd be friends—or not. All that the latter outcome meant was more than I wanted to admit to.

At the end of that trip, we snowshoed up the ridge of a 14,000-foot mountain. Kate got to the top before I made my last oxygen-deprived steps onto the narrow, circular summit. "I can't believe this," I said. The 360-degree view of peaks snow-capped and enormous was one I knew only from postcards. Here the lines were sharper, the cold, thin air a tonic. I began to cry, small definite tears of exhilaration. Kate cried too, and we hugged each other, bundles of Gore-Tex and pile sweaters separating our thin bodies. We held on so long, I felt a rush of cold when Kate finally stepped back and shook her head.

"We're so queer," she said, wiping away a tear before it froze to her freckled cheek.

"No," I said. "You're queer, I'm totally queer." We howled with laughter into the oxygen-thin air and did a stiff-legged dance. At that moment we became the Queer sisters, the Q sisters, Q squared.

This was me and Sue in fourth grade—Sue with whom I joined the Brownies and learned to tie knots between cookie sales. We called ourselves Sue squared. In high school it was Naomi. We rafted and canoed the rivers of central Pennsylvania, hiked the Black Forest Trail. Frick and Frack.

The memory of Sue and Naomi and those long afternoons when we shared our secrets were still my models for friendship, a simple oneness, where we ate, slept, thought the same things. But my early adult years were a desert of female friendships. I knew this was my fault: I was slow to navigate the terrain of female friendship once I came out. I was constantly mistaking potholes for crevasses and backing off long before most people had a chance. But more complicated than the minefield of sexuality was my notion of friendship: if a girl didn't play hard, climb until limp, or hike past exhaustion, I wasn't interested.

Now to my surprise, here was a woman stronger than me, one who waited at the turn in the trail as I worked to keep up. *I had a friend.* The thought thrilled me, but like a schoolgirl, I was afraid that one day she would show up and hand me a neatly folded note that read, *You aren't my friend anymore.*

Before this trip to the Rockies we had jokingly asked each other, "After eight days, will we have anything to talk about?"

"Will you still love me?"

This is how we ski: Kate in front, me behind. It's not something we talk about; it just is. Our pattern makes sense: she's stronger and faster than I am, while I tend to daydream, my thoughts making me drift. We stop frequently to adjust packs and to drink water, to tighten boots, apply moleskin to blisters or hot spots on our feet. If the path is wide enough I ski next to Kate, and we talk. It always surprises me how much we have to talk about. Mostly we discuss friends. Sometimes I feel I know more about her friends than they know about themselves. But as she talks, I listen closely, because in her stories she's worked the pieces of her friends' lives in astonishing ways, and they always come out heroic. When I need a boost, I call Kate. She's also the person I call when I'm tired of my ways. "Q" she says, drawing out the Q, not a warning but a bullshit flag. I listen because I want to understand what it means to be a friend.

● ●

The trailhead had already—miraculously—been broken by a snowmobile. But we weren't skiing side by side or talking as we worked our way toward the first hut. We were trying to beat a storm and the setting sun. I was barely keeping up, and wished that I had trained more, run that hill a few extra times. Three months earlier I had moved in with my lover an hour and a half away, so I hadn't had Kate there to push me as in years past. "I ran out to Awosting," she would report. I knew that run, how it traveled endlessly uphill through rhododendron bushes and oak trees, past one lake then on to another, the sharp views of the craggy New York ridges easing the pain of burning thighs. It was a trail we had run together in the past. Jealous, I laughed, "Good, you can carry my sleeping bag for me."

When we arrived at the hut, the sun was cruising for the horizon, and cold snapped through the pine trees that circled the small wooden building. I threw off my pack, my body springing back as if I might fly. I sat down, watched as Kate dialed the combination of the lock that hung from the massive wooden door of the hut. "Damn," she yelled. I knew what was wrong. We had encountered this before: frozen locks. I started to write a letter in my head to the Tenth Mountain Division about how cheap locks that froze shut were unacceptable. When I looked up from my mental composition, I saw Kate with a large shovel in her hand. She lifted it over her head, landing it squarely on the lock, clanging metal against metal dull and solid. Once, twice, three times. The lock hung limp from the hinge, and I cheered "Go Q."

Our heavy boots thunked against the wooden floorboards, echoing the hollowness of the two-story building. We looked around at the familiar setting, each of the many huts in the Tenth Mountain Division a variation on the basics. The woodstove stood cold in the middle of the room, surrounded by racks for hanging wet clothing. An enormous pile of split wood rested against a near wall, and outside was stacked an even larger pile of unsplit rounds of wood. In the far corner was the kitchen area, three propane burners and a wide assortment of mismatched pots and pans that had no doubt seen several hundred spaghetti dinners. Three long wooden picnic tables lined one side of the cabin. Outside, through the back door and down a narrow tunnel of snow, stood the outhouse, a smelly place even in the deep cold. Upstairs were the sleeping quarters, open rooms with foam-padded bunks and hard pillows. Both of us had brought our own pillowcases.

"Guess we have the place to ourselves," I said. Getting reservations had been so difficult I'd assumed the place would be mobbed. We high-fived each other and then set into a whirl of motion: I fired up the woodstove with the seasoned kindling while Kate figured out how to get the solar-generated lights blazing; I put water on the burners for tea or hot chocolate while Kate headed back out into the cold with a large white plastic bucket to gather snow to melt for more water; I selected rice and dried vegetables for dinner while Kate pulled out the first of the Sunday *New York Times* crossword puzzles, our night-time entertainment.

Then we stripped. We pulled off every layer until I stood in my blue sports bra, and Kate was naked, her breasts exposed as perfect half moons in the dull light that reflected off the walls of the wooden cabin.

"Hey, where are those baby wipes?" I asked.

"You have them," Kate reminded me. Everything was in neat plastic bags, the weight divided evenly between the two of us. It would take a few days before we knew who carried the toothpaste, the cashew nuts, the extra handwarmers. We each had one wipe a day, no more.

"What first?" Kate asked.

"Armpits first," I explained, my voice high-pitched like an airline stewardess at altitude. I made exaggerated motions, demonstrating exactly how to wipe. "Then your dark spot. Once you are nice and clean down there," I continued, "move on to your face. If you feel it necessary you can start over again. Armpits. Dark spot. Face." We laughed at our own idiocy, the joke of how to wipe *just so* a remnant from an earlier trip.

Kate snapped a picture, me with my hip thrown out, long torso swiveling to the side, while I looked down at my hairy armpit, wiping away the sweat of our first day.

The next day we skied from the hut, exploring a nearby mountainside. But our hopes for steep slopes so we could do telemark turns were buried by the new snow. Over two feet of powder made any sort of speed or turns impossible. During the four hours we explored the surrounding woods, the sun never pierced through the clouds or the tightly huddled aspen trees. The light sprinkling of snow never stopped. As we headed back to the hut I cheered at the prospect of warmth and dryness.

From a distance, we could see them: stray skis poking out of the snow at random angles.

"Company," Kate said.

We examined the skis to get a sense of our hut mates. One pair of serious wide telemark skis looked brand-new. Two pairs of beaten backcountry skis. Then one rental pair.

We never knew who we were going to meet in the huts. One year we sat chatting around the woodstove, swapping stories when a woman asked, "If you guys are from New Paltz, do you know Sue Rogers?" I looked at her, baffled. We had climbed together six years earlier in Connecticut, had even corresponded for a few years, exchanging tales of lovers or of climbing and adventure. Kate's list of chance reencounters was much longer than mine, and every year we met someone she had spoken to on a previous trip. She always remembered them first. "How is your son?" she asked one older man from two years earlier. His son had been ill then. "You remember my son?" he asked.

I counted on these random hut mates for entertainment, for stories, for giving me more to share with Kate.

This crew appeared motley: three men and a woman, coworkers united in a passion for physical endurance. One guy, a competitive triathlete, had never been on backcountry skis with a pack on his back before. The rental ski guy. He had arrived and marched upstairs to the bunks. We didn't meet him until he emerged red-faced the next morning.

During the evening, Kate and I huddled over our crossword puzzle, carefully filling in the boxes and listening in on their conversation. We learned they were going the same way we were, on to the Peter Estin hut. "Let's leave early," I suggested. But when we woke the next morning we couldn't open the front door of the hut. Two more feet of snow had fallen. We needed them to break trail to the next hut.

Monica took the lead, breaking trail from the cabin. We followed single file. After twenty minutes, I took the lead, stepping high to break through the light new snow, my weight sinking down deep until my skis disappeared. Slowly, we traversed wide fields then slid into the woods, uphill then down into narrow gullies. Each one of us took turns out front, breaking trail for twenty-minute intervals until we were panting, our thighs on fire from the high-step exertion, and we let the line pass.

From the rear of the pack, the parallel lines of the skis looked solid, almost neat. But even at the back I felt tired, weighed down, my pack digging into my hips and straining my shoulders. I kept fiddling with the adjustments, but nothing helped ease the pain.

In high school, when Naomi and I backpacked together, we would slip rocks into each other's packs, increasing the weight little by little. I'd laugh until she caught on. I knew Kate wouldn't sneak rocks into my pack, because our concern for weight was too serious. But I did think she'd given me more than my share of the food to carry. I let her know.

"No I didn't," she said looking puzzled.

Instantly, I felt petty.

Kate and I didn't get to talk much for the rest of the day, her out in front, me in the middle of the lineup, then me out in front and her toward the back. It was nine hours, nonstop, and I wasn't the only one dragging. It was me and the three boys. By the end of the day, Monica and her trunklike legs, then Kate with her bean poles were up front doing our hard work for us. Seemingly inexhaustible, Kate led for the last forty-five minutes as we slogged uphill in the dark, our headlamps outlining the frozen shapes of pine trees bent from the wind. I stopped twice during that time, once to put on another layer of clothing, and again to slip handwarmers into my gloves. My body was so depleted, not even our motion could keep me warm.

At the Peter Estin hut the solar lights burned brightly, and the small crowded cabin smelled of meat, noodles, sweat. Still fully dressed in three layers of polypro and a huge Gore-Tex parka, I slowly bent my frozen, stiff limbs and folded onto a wooden bench. The woodstove was surrounded by dozens of wool socks, huge boots inclined toward the warmth of the fire. Behind me was an enormous glass window that looked out on the endless night sky, the stars so bright they too looked frozen.

Nearby I overheard one man say to another, "Well, I guess it won't just be gays here tonight." I felt a rush of excitement. And then I thought how odd that was, that my gay and outdoor lives— that usually ran parallel—were intersecting here at 12,000 feet. Looking around the room I was astonished that all these butch-looking men might be gay. Slowly, other conversations filtered into my frozen ears: "my wife," and "the kids." I realized I had heard wrong—it was "guys," not "gays." I stayed by the fire, staring without focus. I could hear Kate's voice in the corner, wondered if possibly she was making friends.

Kate appeared, her face flush from the heat and the wind and cold of the day. She sat down next to me on the narrow wooden bench, her body pushing against my own and whispered in my ear, "The testosterone is toxic."

I nodded and rolled my eyes, aping one of Kate's mannerisms. Then laughter floated out of us like relief. I leaned over to poke at the fire, and tried to stifle a serious bout of the giggles that felt like grade school when it was boys against girls and we knew, before we even began, that we had won.

After dinner, I wedged myself into a seat at a wooden table in the corner, away from their pot of beef stew, their bottles of wine and beer. Kate slipped into the seat across from me. She was already in her hut outfit, light cotton pants, black with white polka dots, that hung loosely on her narrow hips.

"You know, I think you did have more weight today," Kate said.

I looked at her and said, "No I didn't." If ever Kate and I have a fight I want it to be over something that matters. I knew how little things could become big things—those were the fights I had with lovers. The small represented the large. But weight? There's never been a moment when Kate didn't pull all her weight—and then some. If I had loaded more of the food into my pack, it was entirely by accident. A goof. Nothing more.

"It was just a really hard day," I said. "Thanks for breaking the trail."

"We all broke trail," she said.

"Bullshit."

Kate pulled out the now half-finished crossword puzzle. But I spent so little time with men that I sat sipping tea and watched, fascinated by how bad they smelled, how much they ate, how they never seemed to stop moving. But I also admired their long legs and tight butts, and the easy way they patted each other on the back and openly and proudly discussed their wives.

As the night and their drinking wore on (how much did a case of beer weigh, I wondered), one by one they came over, propped a leg on our table, offered us cookies. Suddenly I felt suffocated in the thin beer-warmed air. Kate started talking about her husband and the outdoor store he owned. Her words surprised me, but then I caught on—the emphasis fell heavily on "husband" as if he might be lounging upstairs.

"Your husband lets you go away by yourself like this?" one asked.

I looked away so I wouldn't start laughing.

"So, what do you think?" Kate asked. "Should we go on to Polar Star hut or stay here?" We had been debating off and on for hours whether to continue with our plan or stay at the Estin hut and ski out early.

"Are you kidding?" The men looked at us in disbelief. "You are choosing whether to stay here and tear up some of the best bowls in the Rockies or trudge on to Polar Star?"

To them, the decision was obvious, and pure pleasure principle. For us, it was more complicated. First, there was the weather. There had been too much snow—about two feet at regular timed intervals—and if it continued in this way we might get stuck at Polar Star. Layered on top of the weather were secondary concerns: my health (I was recovering from a long bout of Lyme disease), and Kate's health (she had thrown out her back two days before the trip). We could have tempered these concerns if the snow stopped, at least for a day. But we did have reservations, a plan, and in this sense both of us are good girls, playing by the rules. What if a large party showed up?

"You could sleep on the benches here," one guy suggested. "No one's going to mind having two women stay on with them." They all laughed.

Meanwhile, Kate's parents were waiting in Keystone, no doubt reading about the snowfall and worrying. Their worry translated to our own, and the variables of danger seemed to be working at odds. Reluctantly we decided to stay on, though I wondered silently if we were being too cautious. Doing the whole trip, making it to Polar Star, seemed important, necessary. To *us*.

Kate and I strapped on our skis and weaved down the bowl below the hut, practicing our telemark turns. The run was steep and long enough to allow half a dozen turns before leveling out at the bottom. On our first run I watched Kate head downhill, execute two smooth turns, her knee tucked in tight and low before she hit a pile of snow, a wake left by one of the boys. She sailed onto her face. I followed her, and knocked over in the same sudden way.

The hillside was so carved into beautiful loops that we decided to head out further, find our own fresh powder. Slapping on our skins, we trudged forty-five minutes to the top of the mountain that sat to the east, towering about the hut. Stepping slowly uphill, the tightness burned in my legs from the ski of the day before. Actually, my legs felt rather like steel rods covered with jelly that might give at any moment.

The top of the mountain was wind packed, slick like ice. Kate skated off the top, sunk into her first turn, then the next. Delicious deep powder made for elegant wide loops. She reached the bottom then looked up as she always does and called out, "That's it Q!" just as I face-planted into the snow. "That was great," she howled. I screamed with laughter then dusted myself off. "Really sink down," she coached. "That's it." My pathetic turns, drawn more by gravity and good snow than by technique, still made me glow.

Above, the sky was a perfect blanket of blue after what seemed like endless white and gray. Intoxicated, we skied up and down that mountain four times, so far past exhaustion we mistook our numbness for feeling alive.

After five hours of fun, all I could think of as I skied up to the hut was taking a nap. Outside the hut a colony of backcountry skis stuck up out of the snow like a row of fence slats. I stopped skiing, let my disappointment sink in. "We've got company," I said.

As if we had knocked, two guys stepped out the front door. One was dark haired, short, walking with heavy, long strides that spelled out purpose. He zipped up his blue fuzzy vest, where his name, JAROD, and TENTH MOUNTAIN DIVISION were emblazoned on his chest.

"Where are you ladies spending the night?" he asked.

I looked at Kate. Exhaustion lodged in my throat, choked me. Kate looked at her skis, then up at the sky. "I guess not here."

Jarod started to lecture us about reservations, about how his group had a right to the whole hut. We should have followed our plans to go on to Polar Star, but if we really couldn't go on we could stay.

"You would have to listen to me preach all night," he warned.

That would not be a sermon about forgiveness.

Without discussion we tossed food, clothes, and sleeping bags into our packs and set out at 2:30. In front of us was a seven-hour ski.

We zigzagged down the initial steep hill, speed making it a joyous blue-sky ride. When we started back up the wide trail on the other side of the valley toward Polar Star, we were confident of our path, since we had skied this route two years before. The swish of our skis pushed us forward, the rhythm took over. I skied next to Kate, as she told stories about other trips gone wrong. Nights in the dark, climbs that didn't end, fingers so numb you thought they'd never work again. The idea was to encourage me, or to convince me this wasn't so bad. But the opposite effect was taking hold: I was beginning to imagine this might get worse; our trail might never end.

The sun went down and although Kate pulled out her head-lamp, we continued to ski by the light of the stars and the moon. The result was inevitable: in the darkness, we lost our bearings, wandered around for hours traversing that mountainside in an exhausted daze.

We both loved the thrill of sore muscles. But this, perhaps, was too much.

At nine that night, just when we had decided we might give up and spend the night huddled in our sleeping bags in the woods I pulled out the map one last time. We both stared as if we had never seen a map before. A glaze in Kate's eyes worried me. Then she glanced up and there was a trail marker, a beacon. That small blue dot helped to crack through our frozen skulls to one moment of reason. The hut had to be further *up* the mountain, and we had been skiing in circles venturing onto trails on the middle of the mountain. We headed uphill along a narrow tunnel of a trail. Bushes reached out and swatted us, small dips in the dark made me lurch. Each time I was sure I would go down—and never get back up again.

Within half an hour we saw the hut, silent, brooding in the moonlight. For once, I wished there were other people there, that the hut was warm and lit, inviting.

Operating in slow motion, we turned on lights, settled in. My only real concern was that the fire start quick and hard. Too tired to eat, we lay down next to the woodstove, swallowing the warmth. I couldn't find a position where my body didn't ache. Awed at our own exhaustion, we moaned our pain, made each other laugh at how in trying to avoid overexerting ourselves we'd just skied for twelve hours.

"What an asshole," Kate marveled for the umpteenth time. "Can you imagine tossing two people out of a hut at two thirty in the afternoon?"

I didn't respond. She was right, but silently I was thanking Jarod.

"In the winter," I added. My outrage rested on the surface. Inside, a sense of wholeness filled my heart, the only part of my body that, exempt from pain, could register sensation.

"But I'm glad we did this," I said.

"The Q sisters do it again," Kate said.

We lay in silence. Soon, we gave up pretending to sleep. We

read books left in the hut, and at three A.M. hunger stormed in. Turning on all the lights as if for a party, we warmed tortillas in butter with brown sugar.

The next day we stacked wood, ate pancakes with walnuts and raisins, tortillas smeared with cashew butter. Our food stash was nearly exhausted; the tortillas were crumbled and the noodles looked dull. We both took mini-baths using a basin in the sink, then wandered around half-naked in the overheated hut before slipping back into our sweat-drenched clothes.

Kate demonstrated how she could make her hair stick in any position.

"Oh, lovely, darling. Your hair looks lovely."

My short hair stood straight up from my head. "Maybe we should bring shampoo next time," I suggested.

"Too heavy," she said. She sat at one of the wooden picnic tables, and I realized she was bent over a map, drawing a route of our next trip.

HIMALAYAN COMPANIONS

••

Jean Gould

Before Gertrude Schmidt telephoned at the beginning of April that year to discuss the possibility of our traveling together to a remote Himalayan kingdom, I knew only that she was German, seventy, and lived in the British Virgin Islands. Spring was late in New England, and as her heavy accent came over the wire, thick stalks of coneflowers and yarrow came to mind. Over the years they competed with invading patches of raspberry for control of my garden.

"Who are you?" she said. "And what have you done with your life? How many times have you been to Asia? Why Bhutan? Are you a Buddhist?" I imagined Gertrude's surefootedness over narrow mountain passages, a sturdy frame held by legs that were long and muscular. Her voice was that certain.

At the time Bhutanese tourism was nationalized and restricted to group travel with authorized guides. Many areas were off limits. Determined that the country would not be ruined by foreigners as

Nepal had been, the government avowed that tourism would never be a major source of its economy. Gertrude and I, it appeared, were a "group" of two. A Buddhist travel agency in Ohio made the arrangements for the "pilgrimage," as Gertrude called it.

Himalayan life suited me, I told her. The harsh extremes and delicate balances offered a perspective about the natural world that was not available in the West. Reducing my possessions to what I could carry was liberating. "Possessions can own a person," I said.

A Buddhist, Gertrude reminded me that Bhutan was the one country in the world where Buddhism was the official state religion. Medieval temples and monasteries attracted her; she hoped to arrange an audience with a *Rinpoche,* a high-ranking monk. Having left Germany after the war, she and her physician husband had settled in Washington and had only recently retired to Virgin Gorda.

I liked to think then that I took people as they were. The sixteen-year age difference between us seemed of little consequence; anyone drawn to that part of the world would be a fine companion. When Gertrude ended the call without additional conversation I assumed that she found me acceptable.

But when we met the following October in Nepal, her stature was so dissonant with the voice I remembered that my throat locked against speech. Pale skin and hair made her colorless against tan clothes. The powerful woman, the tall woman I expected had delicate features and was more than half a foot shorter than I. Would she be able to climb above the tree line?

On our flight to Paro in Bhutan, in a plane that nearly grazed the Himalaya, my concerns faded. Gertrude's determination was larger than her body and whatever strength it carried. We had similar independent natures and nonadventurous husbands. She had studied sculpture; I dabbled as a Sunday painter. Our lives appeared to be driven by a need for new experience. As we landed I noted that her jaw line was strong and angular, much like my favorite grandmother's who also had a no-nonsense approach to life. I would not have to carry this woman on my back.

My days in Kathmandu before Gertrude arrived had been melancholy. Although the Himalayan sky sparkled against purple mountains and the clarity of light remained unchanged, the dusty streets were littered with more garbage than I recalled from earlier trips. And the number of automobiles made breathing a strenuous ordeal due to air pollution. Like many others, I wore a surgical mask on Hindu streets, where cows were now absent but beggars were not. Nonetheless my spirits lifted when I bicycled away from the city, through the valley, and into the countryside. Watching a woman and two small children scrub laundry with stones by a stream, I was forced to admit that in the years since I'd climbed among the Annapurna and Everest foothills I'd romanticized the Himalaya. The grandeur of mountains fosters that, of course, but the truth is there's nothing easy or beautiful about the daily struggles marked by poverty.

Clean, almost-sterile Bhutan appeared more like Switzerland than any of its neighbors. Tshering Jamtsho, our state-approved guide, turned out to be a tall, dignified young man who had studied in India and Germany. He wore argyle knee socks just below the hem of his *gho,* a traditional robe. Like many Bhutanese men, he had a moustache. But it was his gleaming teeth that made him so handsome and his straightforward demeanor that convinced me we were in safe hands.

The first evening Gertrude and I stayed in a huge mountainside hotel just outside Thimphu, the capital. We took photographs of each other at dinner in the well-appointed dining room to mark the beginning of our journey. We were the only guests in the entire place.

As we set out the following morning, Tshering claimed a funeral we witnessed by the roadside was auspicious. I believed him. "We leave sins with corpse," he said, "so mind remains clear." A cook and a driver, Pasan and Namgay, sat in front of the government Land Rover with our guide while Gertrude and I occupied the middle seat, giggling when rocks or gullies in the road threw us up and down. The medieval garb of handwoven cloth—robes for men like Tshering's and long dresses or *kiri* for women, mandatory for the Bhutanese—swept us into another era. That first week driving east, we stopped for day hikes and picnics in virgin forests and spent most nights in guesthouses, where Gertrude sunk into a thick blanket roll and I roasted in a new down sleeping bag. Up to 8,000 feet, the air stayed warm after sundown, although by dawn our breath appeared in clouds before us. Pasan, the cook, brought warm water with our tea each morning. While I spent time in the rolling hills with Namgay giving me the names of trees, Gertrude went off with Tshering in search of local monks. The fact that the Ohio agency had registered us as certified Buddhists enabled Tshering to get permits for entry to historic shrines and temples. If my convent upbringing ended with a certain skepticism about loaves and fishes, I nonetheless carried with me a special reverence for the miracles of nature. Although at fifty-four I was ten years beyond the average Bhutanese life span, my companion was revered as if she carried magic in her being. We joked about her higher calling at evening meals. Our days fell into a comfortable rhythm, and we looked forward to the nightly exchanges when we wove the threads of separate afternoons into one piece, making it possible for each of us to be in two places at once.

As we chattered long after midnight, the details of Gertrude's life emerged. In 1939, the year of my birth, she turned sixteen and was sent by Hitler's Youth Corps north to the Polish border to work on a pig farm where untamed horses bit her and men pawed at her innocence. "I could have refused," she said, "but then there would have been no chance to go to university. The war was tough on us."

I remember she paused after this last sentence, and I wondered if she were issuing a challenge. But my own husband had fought in the Philippines, and I decided to say nothing. Later she told me how difficult it was after the war when her job was to interview prisoners on the losing side. I quieted the memory of my six-year-old self dancing in the streets and changed the subject. Although my mother's family came from Berlin in the nineteenth century, I was permitted to shred newspaper for confetti in anticipation of Germany's surrender.

The next day I set off on a trek alone with Tshering and Pasan. At the last minute, Gertrude decided to remain in the Bumthang valley with Namgay. "I don't really need to go," she said. "You'll tell me everything when you get back." Waist-high marigolds surrounded the guesthouse where she would stay. As I slipped the backpack over my shoulders, I commented that the blossoms would taste like liquid gold. She laughed. I hoped she would be all right.

At 10,000 feet the combination of human silence and the voices of nature—nutcrackers harvesting seeds for the winter, blue pines dropping their needles—sharpened my senses. We had picked up a horseman on the way who led two of his charges laden with our packs. At night, as I prepared to fall asleep in caves or occasionally in a tent, I missed Gertrude and our evenings of easy banter. When I crossed aqua glacial streams on narrow logs, I hoped I'd remember to tell her about the eddies swishing beneath me. But as we got to higher altitudes my stride became a walk of delayed small steps: one foot—stop—then the other—stop. Pushing beyond my means required total focus on the present, making me always more alive. Jolts of primary colors of sky and flora among mountain passes offered no transition, and the angularity of fields against walls of massive stone can set a mind reeling, challenging one's equilibrium. Now and again the horseman cleared one of his animals so I could ride when light faded. The gentle rocking rendered my body limp, and when we reached our camp I rolled off the creature onto a tarp by the fire and escaped the confines of my boots with a sigh. When fatigue precluded appetite one evening I was grateful that Pasan insisted on spoon-feeding me. Before setting out in the morning, I sometimes wondered how I could explain to Gertrude the contentment that flowed through me. She would not approve of my drinking from streams, and find it horrifying that village women touched my breasts, my face, my hair.

When I got back to Bumthang we hugged as if years had passed. I was not surprised. In a place where time is measured by seasons, its linear quality dissolves with no way to rein the hours and days into conventional order. As we engaged more and more with the present, I never got to tell Gertrude about the trek. The following morning we began a climb to Tharpaling, the thirteenth-century monastery where we were scheduled to meet with Lama Nawang Kesang. In preparation, Gertrude had spent three days in a silent retreat. I admired her. I was too restless to sit in one place for very long.

The legend is that parts of Tharpaling had been besieged by demons and had fallen to ruins before the spirits were vanquished. At nearly 12,000 feet, the place was not visible from the mountain's base. Indeed, the slope to the monastery was so steep that the two of us grimaced acknowledging the impossibility of the task before us.

"Don't worry," said Tshering. "This is gentle slope."

"We'll go slowly," I said.

"Of course," said Gertrude, tightening her jaw.

As we started out, a single line of tiny monks with shaved heads skittered down the mountainside. At the rear an older man cracked a whip made of rope with knots at its end. On Sundays, Tshering told us, the monks bathed in the river. The monk with the whip was the master of education, he said. A long time after that, in midafternoon, the lama, a small man in maroon robes, greeted us at the gate to the magnificent structure, which looked more like a fortress than anything else. He had waited all day for us. Did we get a late start? In fact, the bathers had passed us on their way back to the monastery. Were we all right?

Inside his quarters tea was served in bone china. A tin of shortbread cookies appeared. As Tshering translated, Gertrude and the lama began the first of their metaphysical talks. When I presented him with the hiking boots a devotee from Pittsburgh had asked me to bring, he said, "A promise written on stone is lasting; one written on water is not." The remark had a pivotal quality for me, as if it held the key to something I sought but could not name.

Cross-legged on the wooden floor beside a Swiss stove from the last great war, we spoke in whispers as a powerful wind rising from the mountainside merged with our words. When the lama turned to question me, I smiled. Sitting as he was with the sun behind him, his body took on a yellow glow, and his face was in shadow, making conversation strangely more comfortable for me. I'd grown up in a convent, I told him, with the Sisters of the Sacred Heart. That was, in fact, where my wanderlust originated, less from geography class than from living with refugee children whose parents' whereabouts were unknown. Tshering said there was no Dzongkha word for "wanderlust," and it took a while before I remembered *dragpa*, Tibetan for "nomad." My legs cramped just then. Gertrude and I had ridden horses with wooden saddles partway to Tharpaling, and my knees had hugged the animal when we passed up, and especially down, over the rocky terrain.

At dusk Tshering began to pack our things. But when Gertrude said she couldn't possibly find her way down the mountain in the dark, on or off a horse, I knew she had planned all along to stay overnight.

"Women cannot stay in monastery," Tshering said. "It is not permitted."

"Perhaps the lama might lead us in a meditation before we leave," I said, looking for a neutral place.

"Yes," Nawang Kesang said in English. "A brief meditation."

"We will have peaceful time," said Tshering. "Then go."

In the darkness the temple might have been any musty building with a cold stone floor, yet the lama's intonations took me away from this world. He spoke of compassion and kindness. Afterward as we spread yellow saffron water over our eyes, as was the custom, my vision seemed keener than it had been. When we stepped away from the temple, the lama's assistant said everything was arranged for us to spend the night. Because of her advanced age, Gertrude had prevailed.

Our dinner was served in the lama's quarters while the discussion about Buddhism and all things religious continued. When the lama inquired further about my experience in the convent, the word "Catholic" seemed inappropriate. I'd left organized religion long ago. As canvas shades were rolled over windows, I wondered if the stars were above or below and how bright they would be if I could find them. Uncrossing my legs, the circulation returned as I lengthened them in front of me, an insulting gesture in Bhutan. "I'm sorry," I said.

"It is permitted," said the lama again in the English, emphasizing the *ts*.

Gertrude drank *ara*, a potent alcohol made from barley. There must be some relief for her, I thought, in having her questions about life and its purpose discussed with affection and sincerity. When at last we lay on mattresses and covered ourselves with Hudson Bay blankets, the voices of the others hummed like melodies. We might have been children anywhere listening to adults after our bedtime, knowing we were safe.

Before dawn the chanting of monks from the temple woke us. Rolling the canvas away, I saw that the monastery was clearly above the clouds. Yes. The sun rose beneath us. We soon found ourselves making our good-byes, touching our foreheads to the lama's as he wrapped white *kivas,* ceremonial scarves, around our necks. A photograph shows him standing between Gertrude and me, arms intertwined across our shoulders.

My companion sat on her horse as if it were a throne, and directed the shy boy who had the lead. I fairly flew down the mountainside, stopping just once to admire butterflies whose wings were the color of morning glories. At the bottom I dropped breathless into a meadow of tall grass, stretching arms and legs to all the corners of Bhutan.

Our next destination, Gantey, is the valley where black-necked cranes winter when their Tibetan plateau habitat freezes. Just a day later, on our way there, the trouble began. Looking for raisins in her pack, Gertrude whispered that a gold necklace she had purchased in Delhi was gone and that her money was also missing. When she told Tshering, his head fell onto his chest; he had developed bronchitis in recent days and his energy had waned. Saying nothing about Gertrude's announcement, he related the tale of the Gantey cranes and their devotion to one another. Every winter seven birds arrive early to scout the valley's marshlands; these are also the last to leave when the season ends, attending to wounded birds until they heal. Mating for life, partners sometimes fly with young chicks on their wings. The crane is the bird of happiness.

Rows of cabbage lined the path to the farmhouse where we would spend the night with an elderly couple. Since Buddhism teaches that attachment to things can only lead to unhappiness, I assumed that Gertrude would not be too upset by the loss of her necklace and cash. With more travelers checks than she could ever use, she had nothing to worry about.

"What a shame," I said as we settled ourselves in the main room. "On the other hand, whoever took your things must need them more than you do."

"I must go back and see lama," said Tshering standing at his full height, his arms folded across his chest like a warlord. "I will find necklace."

The driver's face, the cook's face fell as they told the farmer and his wife what had happened. With another Swiss stove from the war, the room grew almost hot, and for the first time Tshering gave instructions for our tea to be plain black instead of the thick yak butter version I found so energizing. With that gesture the situation became a serious one, separating Westerners from Bhutanese. We had just driven twenty-four hours with a brief halt in Tongsa over roads blocked by boulders from landslides. Only one paved passage from east to west existed, and efforts to keep it in repair were constant. Winters froze the blacktop, making cracks, and in May and June monsoons caused mudslides. Retracing our steps would involve a major effort. And we would go at night, something really dangerous, since there were no lights over the hairpin turns. Often large animals, tigers, for example, or wild boars, lay on the road to warm themselves. If we hit one of them we'd be certain to go over the mountain's edge.

Rummaging through her bags, Gertrude murmured to herself. Her clothes now covered chairs, tables, and the rough-hewn hardwood floor. "Maybe I put the necklace in one of my pockets," she said as if she were alone in the candlelit room.

We all spoke at once then, trying to let her know that everything was going to be fine. Even the wife and her husband let it be known that they shared her loss and held their arms out to her. I got up and took her hand in mine, but she pushed me away with such force that I lost my balance and would have fallen had the wife not caught me. And then all of us were standing facing one another.

"The necklace. The necklace," Gertrude shouted, forcing us to look around as if a wild animal had entered the room. "My husband gave me five hundred dollars to buy that necklace."

A uniform gasp filled the space among us. The per capita income in this part of the world was much less than the value of her gold jewelry. A few sparks rose against the flue like small explosions. I didn't want to blame her—she was the victim after all, wasn't she?—but I wondered why she hadn't worn the necklace under her turtlenecks.

"I—need—that—necklace," she said, pausing for seconds between each word.

No one responded. There was no place for a five-hundred-dollar piece of jewelry in this context. So we attended to our own business as if nothing had happened. Tshering and Namgay checked the van's engine. I went out to use the latrine and then threw sticks until the farm dog stopped retrieving them. Pasan in his usual makeshift kitchen built a fire and cooked another superb dinner, this time yak meat with gravy and buckwheat noodles, preceded by a delicious cream of chicken soup. A vegetarian, Gertrude ate only the noodles.

With just the two of us sitting as close to the stove as we could get to ward off the evening chill, Gertrude grew conspiratorial. "Do you remember that horseboy?" she said. "The one with the red mark on his face who led me up to Tharpaling? I didn't like his look," she said. "Sneaky."

The dinner congealed just beneath my esophagus as anger rose quickly, then receded, then rose again. "It's only a thing, the necklace," I said, reaching for the exquisite moment not so very long ago when the lama had led us in a meditation and Gertrude, Tshering, the lama, and I had breathed as one.

"I need my necklace," she said. "Why don't you see that?"

"We can't make Tshering drive back to Bumthang, climb the mountain, wake the lama just to search for a piece of jewelry," I said. If I were in her place I wondered if I would be able to let go of what I considered rightfully mine. I hoped that I would.

When Tshering entered the room with a sober look, coughing, his face flushed with fever, I knew I would have to take a stand. "You must go right to bed," I told him.

"Am I such a failure?" he said to Gertrude. "Shall I go back to Tharpaling? What do you want me to do?"

"Nothing," I said.

"If you don't go," Gertrude fired at him, "I'll go myself."

The notion was preposterous. "And how will you do that?" I said.

"I'll rent a car," she said. "I'll rent a car."

We both knew that neither Avis nor Hertz was around the corner. In fact, few Bhutanese had cars. Gertrude was goading Tshering, playing on his guilt as if it were his responsibility to keep track of her possessions.

In the end, of course, he and Namgay set out alone in total darkness for the monastery. I stayed up until the stove went out, talking with the old couple by way of family photographs. Gertrude went to her room, returning only to demand an electric heater. Obviously she had left Bhutan altogether and had gone to a place where electricity and hot running water were commonplace. I felt sad about the tangle she'd created, but I didn't know how to square that against her imperious expectations.

Gertrude wrote letters home the next day, even though there was no place to post them. Pasan and I roamed fields to the blind where in winter one could view the black-necked cranes in the valley. We walked to Gantey's monastery, which was closed because the lama there was on a three-year-retreat, but the little village surrounding the temple was alive and busy with commerce. I traded a brass ring for an old *mala* (rosary) of sandalwood. When I'd bartered a packet of dried apricots for the ring in Bumthang, Gertrude had said the ring was worthless.

Back at the farmhouse, Pasan and I sat outside with the farmer, who threw stones at the birds and ground animals that were stealing his cabbage. Two-dimensional scarecrows with large metal objects clanged in the wind to keep bears away. If she knew, Gertrude would find the scarecrow idea ingenious; the farmer pointed to the house, reminding me of her whereabouts.

At dinner when I asked how her day had gone, she said she hoped Tshering had found the horseboy with the red mark. After the meal I tried to write a poem, a simple one about the scarecrow, the cabbage field, and the farmer's stones, but I couldn't. When I suggested a walk to Gertrude, she asked if I could keep the farm animals away from her. Virtually all Bhutanese houses had barns on the lower level with living quarters above. When I backed down the ladder nothing stirred. "It's OK," I said, flashing my torch up to her, taking her arm at the elbow.

"At the crane blind," I told her, "I was able to hear the birds getting ready for takeoff."

"Oh Jean," she said, "you don't live in the real world."

Was she joking? As I gripped her forearm to steady her over the uneven ground and we walked to the end of the cabbage patch, I chose to believe that she was. When the scarecrows clanged we sat on a wall by the side of the house. The stars were above us this time.

Long after midnight Tshering and Namgay returned, honking the van's horn until all of us, even Gertrude, went out to greet them. They had driven for twenty-four hours, climbed the mountain, roused the lama, and ultimately recovered the necklace. Tshering lifted a bottle of *ara* from his pack, and we all toasted his successful adventure. The whiskey scalded my throat but I didn't care.

"It was that horseboy, wasn't it?" said Gertrude. "The one with the mark on his face."

Inside the house Tshering confided that all the horseboys were monks in training who were too frightened to steal. If he were caught, a boy would be stripped naked, tied down, and whipped one hundred times by the education master. It seemed, he said, that a slow boy who often hung around the monastery had rifled Gertrude's bag while we meditated in the temple. Hoping to gain favor with others, he had already given the money away. Once discovered, he took Tshering directly to a group of nettle shrubs under which the necklace was hidden. We clapped our hands as Tshering drew it from an inner pocket and lifted it for all to see.

The long chain had no glitter, was ordinary, possibly even a bit more gray than gold. When I thought of it later, I realized that no item could have matched the strain of its recovery.

"We climb mountain to monastery in middle of night," said Tshering. "Without torch. We wake lama who weeps when he hears news. All monks are interrogated."

Gertrude and I, Pasan and Namgay, the farmer and wife shivered in the room with the now-cold Swiss stove while Tshering added details to his story. None in the monastery would admit guilt, and the lama sent every monk down the mountain to find the stolen property. At sunbreak an older monk recalled that the slow boy had been hanging around the monastery that day. An orphan, he hoped to become a monk and often was allowed kitchen scraps. Tshering found the boy later that morning in a field tending cows.

"When I see him," he said, "I know he has guilt. I put belt around him and hang him upside down. I am like Nazi. He take me to necklace."

The Nazi reference was not lost on me. As Gertrude stiffened, Tshering half-winked at me, and I began to wonder which parts of his story were true and which were embellished.

"I hope he will be severely punished," said Gertrude.

"Getting caught, losing face is punishment enough," I said.

Later on Tshering would tell me that he had taken the boy in his arms and said all was forgiven. "He is child," he said.

"Everybody does dumb stuff," I said, meaning the purchase of the necklace more than the boy's transgressions.

In subsequent days without once mentioning the necklace, Tshering and I took great care with one another. He agreed to try the antibiotics I had brought from home, and he quickly recovered. He arranged longer hikes, during which he identified plants used for indigenous medicine. And Gertrude kept up with us. We were both acclimatized at last.

She began talking about going home to Virgin Gorda. Her husband had crippling arthritis, she said, soothed only by warm Caribbean waters. But she was lonely there. Worse, as her husband aged, she found it more and more difficult to get away. If she returned without the necklace, perhaps he would refuse to let her leave again.

I made no comment. I would spend weeks in Kathmandu with friends and then travel to Dharamsala in northern India, the seat of the Tibetan government in exile.

Several years later when Bhutanese tourism was privatized, I returned again and was fortunate to have Tshering as my guide. Gertrude and her husband had moved to the Italian Alps despite his body's need for warmer climes, and the two of us corresponded now and again. She'd had a heart attack, she said, and had given up Buddhism. She had never worn the gold necklace, yet its power to rouse strong feelings in me endured.

On our way across Bhutan during that later trip, Tshering and I stopped at the farmhouse in Gantey where Gertrude and I had waited for the return of her property. In early March only thirteen cranes remained. Each day I went to the blind to watch these elegant birds practice their departure, taking off, circling, and then landing again in the marsh. Cranes had the habit of dancing—bowing, and leaping, tossing vegetation about while trumpeting calls that can be heard miles away. The morning they left for good, three birds rode on the wings of others, and their red crowns provided the only color in Gantey.

DISORIENTING

• •

Kim Todd

We were lost. As we came over the ridge, no doubt remained. The hill, which I had hoped would descend to some landmark once we'd crested it, plunged thickly forested to a frozen lake that didn't appear on the map. Then the ground rose again and green hills bucked all the way to the horizon. Boulders covered the slope behind us—arrested, it seemed, in mid-tumble. The sky was blank, gray, hostile. Roots poked through the soil. Anchored only by a topographical map of the Indian Heaven Wilderness in the South Cascades and a compass that I understood more in theory than in practice, I wondered how far we could go before being found.

Staring at the anonymous hills, I felt unmoored. All the ways I used to locate myself had fallen away. No familiar peak or rock formation told me that I was facing north. No sign directed me to go left or right. I couldn't envision myself standing firmly on a specific point on the map, because we'd veered away from the Pacific

Crest Trail, a 2,700 mile path that stretches from Mexico to Canada. With that well-traveled route left behind, now we were weaving among the topo lines. In some part of my mind, I held a tether that led me back to the house on Hopkins Street in Berkeley where I had grown up. With no road or marked path to follow home, that tether was severed too, as surely as if the golden thread had snapped when Theseus wandered his way through the maze toward the Minotaur. I didn't know how to imagine where I was.

Beside me, clinging to a fistful of grass so she wouldn't slide down the hill, was my friend Karen, whom I called Karenina, because she had a flair for the dramatic. We had bonded during our first semester of college as two Californians struggling on the East Coast. We'd spent the next four years arguing about Shakespeare, writing and directing plays which we performed in dark corners of the college basement, fine-tuning our pasta recipes, crying and wondering why we were so miserable. Karen experimented with her image the way some people experiment with drugs, trying to find the persona that offered the best worldview. One summer I picked her up from a Buddhist meditation retreat in Orinda and was greeted by a woman I hardly knew, round face glowing with inner peace, long cotton skirt flapping around her bare ankles. Another time I met her at the airport. One of the last passengers off the plane, she ran up to greet me, looking like a movie star. Her California-blond hair had gone raw honey brown in the eastern climate, and she was wearing a leopard-skin coat that reached mid-thigh.

On the other hand, when Karen opened the car door or stepped out of a plane, she always knew what to expect from me: the same brown hair just past shoulder length, the same boots, the same willingness to eat peanut butter sandwiches every day for lunch. Despite these differences, we'd stayed in touch after graduation, mainly because one thing about Karen remained constant through all her permutations. I could call her and suggest almost any adventure and she would say yes. When I told her I planned to hike 500 miles on the Pacific Crest Trail through Washington State and asked if she wanted to join me for a portion, she bought a rain suit at Target and got on a plane.

The first three days of hiking were misery. The moment we left the Oregon border and started north, rain poured down from a low-slung sky, pausing every hour or so as if to take a breath, only to continue with renewed force. Our packs were bulky and too heavy, resembling small walruses swathed in nylon. They cut into our shoulders, gaining weight as the water seeped into our clothes and food. Karen, who is just over five feet tall and who cheerfully took my suggestion and ignored the REI guy's advice about how much weight she should carry, grew more and more quiet as each gust of wind threatened to knock her off balance. Summer was coming slowly after a stormy winter had washed out roads and bridges throughout southwest Washington. Though it was late June, buds were still knotted tight as fists.

When the rain eased briefly into mist, my mood lightened and I made conversation.

"What are you thinking about?" I prodded Karen.

"This book I just finished about soldiers on a death march," she said.

We continued on. As the path ran along the side of Berry Mountain, it was easy to follow, but then it moved off the crest into a broad, snow-filled bowl. Trees poked through the white expanse, and we wove around them, making deep footprints so we could find our way back. Finally, it came to this: the trail was gone.

We camped at the spot where the trail disappeared. Dropping snowballs into the pot to melt for dinner, Karen edged around the topic of bailing out on the trip, and I ignored her. Instead, we pondered the nature of wetness and dryness and how the slightest bit of the former can make the latter an impossible dream. We made a list of items we should have left behind: the second pot, binoculars, camp shoes, the second roll of toilet paper, the trowel. We promised never to leave our lovers again, our lovers who were sleeping under clean sheets in large beds, alone. As we talked, the snow on the stove gradually turned into gray slush, then melted into liquid, and then, after what seemed like an hour, kicked up a half-hearted boil.

After a plateful of spaghetti, Karen tried again and pinned me into a conversation about what we would do if the rain continued and the snow obscured the trail for miles ahead. She wanted to retrace our steps to the last road we'd crossed, twelve miles back. But I insisted we go on, reluctant to abandon our plans, confident that we would find the trail tomorrow. In two days my friend Audrey was going to drop off more supplies and have lunch with us where the trail crossed Road 65. We could discuss the future of the trip then, I argued, if we could find the trail to that point. If we couldn't, the map showed that Road 65 was three or four miles west of us, on the other side of a ridge. We could just bushwhack to the top, see the road below us, and make our way down to it. It would be easy.

My confidence sprang from the notion that if we climbed higher than the land around us, we would be able to place ourselves within the view. Vision dominates the human senses, and most people construct their mental maps from what they see, designing charts on a useful, intimate scale. My friend Clara, who doesn't have a car and whose urban instincts don't let her walk alone at night, imagines herself on a grid of bus lines and bus stops. She calculates how close she is to safety and how many rumbling bus rides she is away from home. My boyfriend's landscape is emotional. He locates himself in relation to the house of an ex-lover, the first place he applied for a job, the state where his parents live. Audrey, who grew up on the Oregon coast and now lives in Seattle, envisions herself in relation to bodies of water. In Seattle she sits perched on the land bridge between Lake Washington and Puget Sound, too far away to feel the tug of the ocean. All these maps are unique, idiosyncratic, and they all rely primarily on sight.

But other animals locate themselves by sound, smell, vibrations, or senses we don't fully understand. I once heard a story about a boy who collected migrating birds injured during a storm. The high winds blew the birds into a power line and they fell to the ground, stunned. The boy put them in the back of his car and drove them to a nearby animal shelter. By the time he arrived, most of the birds had recovered, and when he opened the trunk, they were all facing, not the back of the car, not each other, but due south. The healthy birds flew off as soon as they were free, and even the ones that couldn't fly hopped out of the car and started walking south. The boy grew up to be an ornithologist, specializing in navigation.

Some say birds follow the stars as they migrate thousands of miles each year. One group of scientists put indigo buntings in a star chamber, then revolved the stars, so south was no longer south, west no longer west. The birds shifted accordingly, reading the false stars rather than true north. Other people say birds use the sun or the topography of mountain ranges and coast lines to find their way. Scientists have sought to prove pigeons navigate by gauging the earth's tilt and the resulting geomagnetic forces. Pigeons wearing magnets (which disrupted their internal compass) had difficulty returning to their loft on cloudy days when they couldn't navigate by the sun. Birds with brass bars instead of magnets managed to find their way home, even under overcast skies. Photopigment in the pigeons' eyes may translate magnetic fields as well as light, telling birds whether they are flying toward a pole or toward the equator.

Anyone who has watched Canada geese "V"ing overhead or heard their distant calls in the dark knows that there is a confidence in these strong, sure, wing beats, a confidence that we seem to lack.

The next morning I left Karen at the tent, wool hat pulled far over her ears, reading the passage on hypothermia in my first-aid book. As I put on my boots, I saw, not a hundred yards from our tent, a Pacific Crest Trail marker. And then another, on the inside of a tree. Soon I was strolling through the snow, barely breaking stride to look for markers or melted-out patches of trail. I found Blue Lake, cold water lapping at the base of Gifford Peak, and ran back to tell Karen. But when we returned with our packs and pressed beyond the lakeshore, the trail vanished again into ice and twigs and confusion. If we needed to hunt for the trail every hundred yards, we would average three miles a day and miss Audrey completely. After trying three times to cross an ice-clogged stream, we agreed to bushwhack.

When I suggested cutting away from the trail, I didn't think it necessary to plot a compass point. But for form's sake I placed the edge of the compass on the map so it ran a straight line from Blue Lake to the road, then I turned the dial so the direction lines on its face were parallel with our chosen path. When I lifted the compass off the map and held it so the needle pointed north, an arrow on the dial pointed us the way we should walk. But it wasn't the direction that I sensed was west.

We started to follow the arrow against my instincts, and I adjusted the compass, holding it flat and noting a landmark near where it pointed. We would then walk to that landmark, and adjust the compass again. Our progress was slow and methodical. Tree to tree to tree. Big Douglas fir to small clump of cedar to twisted stump split by lightning. Moving sometimes five feet, sometimes twenty-five, we inched in the direction we hoped was west. At first I offered to show Karen how to use the compass, so we could alternate guiding. She plunged ahead, through bushes and over logs, holding the bearing out like a divining rod. But after two legs she handed the instrument back to me.

"I'm not having control issues here," she said. "You can lead."

When the compass directed us over a frozen lake, I stayed on one shore with the bearing, while Karen went around, heading for the marked spot on the opposite bank. As I sat on my pack, feet in the snow, holding the compass, which I pointed over the lake to a clump of trees, I heard a yelp. Then Karen's shaky voice.

"I'm all right."

She had fallen through the ice and sunk in the water up to her hip. Back onshore, she waved back at me and pressed on. Then another scream. Then a pause.

"I'm okay." The words quavered over the ice.

Fortunately, the day remained warm, through not sunny, and Karen's waterproof pants dried as we walked. Past evergreen trees tipped with tender new needles. Past quick streams connecting a small chain of lakes. I felt a flush of privilege at seeing sights not on the trail, not on the designated tour, and I remembered a man I knew who scorned hiking trails in favor of walking a compass line. Hiking for him was plotting a course and plunging forward down hills and over stumps until he grew tired, then turning 180 degrees and heading back. He returned from these jaunts full of stories of coyote pups squealing in their dens and moose knee-deep in muddy pools. But I declined his invitations, favoring the trail and gathering a quiet joy from stumbling across a mileage sign. And now that I had veered from the path, the thrill of off-route exploring was blotted out by my persistent fantasizing about the road. Over and over in my mind I crested the mountain, saw the blacktop, felt the flood of relief.

Finally, after we had walked out of the snow, across a slick rock field, past dozens of melting ponds, we crossed over the ridge. Instead of the anticipated view down to the paved road, we saw the boulders at our feet, the hills that went nowhere. To our right the ridge curved, and when I checked the compass, it pointed us across the steep slope and back to the other side. That couldn't be right. Discouraged, I sat down for a break. What were we supposed to do? A new plan? I was out of plans. My hands shook, rustling the plastic bag with our food in it as I tried five times to undo the knot. Blood beat in my ears, making it hard to hear my thoughts over the static. All decisions seemed equally wrong, all directions equally fruitless. I ate the last of my graham crackers and peanut butter and wished I could cry to loosen, if only slightly, the bands of anxiety that had wound themselves around my chest. Karen had already cried twice, saying, "I'm going to cry now, but it's okay, Kim, I just do this sometimes. I don't want you to think that I'm not having a good time." And she would sob, and the rain would drip off the tree branches and run down the inside of our rain gear, and I would try to think of comforting things to say, and fail.

My problem was a crisis of faith. Deep down, I didn't believe in the compass, this small circle that claimed to describe our world. It was plastic. It had cost fifteen dollars. How was it going to save us?

We were far from the trail, I knew that, and the likelihood of anyone finding us was slim. But despite the tears, Karen was confident. Maybe beneath her shifting personae she was more certain of her direction than I was. Maybe by changing variables so often she knew more about the constants. She trusted the compass. And I think she trusted me. I trusted neither and could only avoid panic by never stopping long enough to think. We stood up and prepared to go back over the ridge. Tree to tree to tree.

When I imagine a landscape more disorienting than rows of hills, I think of the ocean. Undulating planes of color reflecting the blue or gray or black of the sky. Before compasses and Geographic Information System and satellite photography, sailors would set out with knowledge of the wind and stars to help them home. At sea, Greek mariners knew where they were by the smell and feel of the wind that blew behind them or in their faces. Boreas, the north wind, was the coldest, while Notus came from the south and blew warm weather. The heavy wet breeze from the west was termed Zephyr. Apeliotes raged from the east. The stars also acted as a map, and if the rolling waves looked monotonous and the night was clear, sailors could look up and key on Polaris, the anchor of the sky.

When someone noticed that a needle rubbed with a magnet stone would point north, early mariners made their first progress toward the compass. They secured the needle to a piece of wood, floated it in a bowl of water, and followed its lead. It seemed more magical than scientific, but it cast a reliable spell. Sailors thought the needle pointed to the North Star rather than the North Pole, but either way, it guided them into port. As time passed, inventors modified the needle, enclosing it in a case inscribed with sixty-four directional points.

This tool, the compass, makes up for our flaws: our dependence on vision, our optimism. Psychological experiments show that when most people walk through a neighborhood then map it, they draw an idealized picture. They make acute angles right and straighten twisted streets. Without help from an objective source, they amend the landscape to their specifications. When the fictional scene intersects the actual, people become disoriented.

Even the word "orient" varies between the directional and the personal. Originally, it named the direction where the sun rises, the east. The word worked itself from a Latin verb meaning "to rise," to a noun describing a section of sky, back to a verb as worshipers built their churches with the altar in the east and buried their dead with the feet facing east. "Orient" eventually started to describe the placement of people, not just temples and tombs. To orient yourself was not only to know where you were in relation to the four cardinal points; it was also to know which way to point your prayers, to understand who you are.

After pushing through underbrush that snagged our packs and scratched our arms, Karen and I followed our bearing into a grove of tall Douglas fir. Though the ground had appeared level for the past hour, we must have been gradually descending, because we started walking through spring rather than winter. While our eyes stayed trained on the thick-ribbed bark, we couldn't help but notice the flowers on the ground and the rich smell of green. Raindrops from a recent shower clustered on petals and leaves. Then I looked up, and saw that the trees ended. Instead of more hills, they were backed by a wall of sky. Karen thought we must be at a cliff. I had a brief image of a steep concrete drop-off bordering the interstate. But what we were seeing was simply distance. After focusing so closely for hours, our eyes couldn't make sense of the miles of unobstructed view that opened up as we came to the end of the trees. We were almost in the clearing before I could see that the hazy planes of white and brown and green composed a mountain so large that it defined the landscape around it. A snow-covered cone whose shoulders ranged in all directions. A crater full of clouds. Pebbles on the ground, light as popcorn and blasted with holes. All the signs said this was Mount St. Helens. A landmark.

We stood at the boundary of a wilderness area, at the point where the shady understory of the tall trees was replaced by a sun-raked clear-cut, dotted with saplings only knee- and shoulder-high. And at the base of the clear-cut, separating it from another logged area by twenty-odd feet, a stripe of gravel coursed from north to south. Road 65.

After not trusting the compass, now I didn't trust my eyes, and I followed the bearing all the way out to the road. Though it was smaller than the highway of my imagination, and was bordered by horsetail and yellowed grass, it led to bigger roads and an entire network of known streets and neighborhoods. With Mount St. Helens towering to the west and the gravel under our feet, we stood firmly on the map. With enough charts placed side by side, we could find our way to San Francisco, Chicago, or New Orleans from this point, and the knowledge of this connection thrummed through me like blood. Confidence surged back. I put down my pack and ran up a slight hill to where the road curved to see if I could find the corresponding curve on the map and pinpoint our location exactly. Karen scooped up a handful of gravel and ran it through her fingers as though it were the bread crumbs set down by Hansel and Gretel. Loping back, I swept Karen up in a hug. Then we flopped on our packs in the middle of the empty dusty road and stared up at the sky. The smooth blue curve seemed friendly again.

The story doesn't end with the simple success of our navigation or the simple failure of our journey. Four days and several more adventures lay between us and showers in Seattle. When we finally arrived in Seattle, Karen declared the trip over and flew home to pursue more urban ventures. But she still says yes, always yes, when I propose an expedition, though she now asks first, "How cold will it be?" I, more willing now to step outside the boundaries of my original plan and cross the lines I'd drawn for myself, rethought my trip and rejoined the Pacific Crest Trail. Two months later, footstore and exhilarated, I stepped into Canada. The rest of the hike offered thunderstorms, hissing bear cubs, and wild blueberries by the fistful, but my memories of that summer always converge on the moment when the compass pointed placidly to the road, and I glimpsed a world beyond what my senses could paint for me, a world with a logic larger than my own. In that instant, my mental map stretched to a different scale, and I believed briefly and fervently in a planet with magnetic poles, scored by lines marking longitude and latitude; then the valley closed in, the wind picked up, and Karen and I started north to set up camp for the night.

MIKE

• •

Gretel Ehrlich

Mary Francis Tisdale Hinckley came to my door the day I moved into a log house on Trapper Creek in northern Wyoming and asked if I wanted to cowboy with her the next morning. She was tall and elegant, a blue-eyed fifty-five-year-old with nervous hands, which is why, she said, she had to smoke. She wore tight Levi's with a crease pressed in, a gray-and-white striped cowboy shirt, silver earrings, and a silver ponytail that swung under her Stetson. She wasn't a complete stranger. I had known her nephew who lived in another town, and he'd told her that I wanted to ride.

At five A.M. she pulled in with a horse trailer. "Load up," she said, but when she saw my old horse, Blue, she looked dismayed. He was a hairy-legged sheepherder horse with a roman nose and ears almost as long as a donkey's. We were going to help neighboring ranchers, Stan and Mary Flitner, move their cattle from spring pasture to the high country where they would spend the summer. Halfway up the mountain, "Mike" as she was called, finally said,

"Where'd you get that horse? From a sheepherder? God, we've got to find you something better looking."

Mike had grown up on a big Wyoming ranch on the Powder River out of Kaycee. She knew men who "would saddle a horse to go a hundred yards, just to get a cup of water," and her favorite motto was, "If it can't be done horseback, it ain't worth doing." Her other favorite expression, yelled out at dances, was, "Powder River, let 'er rip!" At all other times, however, she was a perfect lady.

After attending the University of Wyoming for two years, Mike went home to the 3T Ranch where her father was foreman. He said, "Well, if you're going to come home and ride with the men, you better make a hand out of yourself."

And she did. Her brother Tommy Tisdale recalled, "That first year she didn't know how to rope, and the first time we had to delouse the cattle we gave her the ground job wrestling cattle. At the end of the day she asked for my rope, and by the next time we had to work cattle she was heading and heeling in the corral."

The 3T Ranch where Mike and Tom grew up was set in low rolling hills with the snow-capped Big Horn Mountains to the west. Out on the plains, the Powder River flowed. "It made for a bad ice crossing in the winter and quicksand in the summer," she always told me. "It was an all-around sonofabitch, but it didn't matter—it was water. We called the high country where we took the cattle in the summer 'Siberia.'"

Mike's favorite horses were Jimmy Jump and Buster Brown. "Once a calf ran back and ended up down below us. That Buster Brown horse came around hard and jumped down six feet off the cliff. He wasn't going to let that steer get by. We got him turned."

Mike rode in what is now historic outlaw country. Some of those outlaws were her relatives who had come north from Texas with the trail herds after the Civil War. "It was good grass country. The rustlers—some were my great uncles—wintered cattle in the canyons by the Outlaw Cave. The ranchers didn't even know they were there. In the spring of the year they'd take the cattle out through the Hole-in-the-Wall and go down to Arminto, and south into Utah from there."

At the top of the mountain we unloaded the horses, saddled them, and rode through timber to the pasture where the cattle were grazing. "We'll bring these up to the dirt road, follow it for a few miles, then cut off, and take them up that draw," Mike said. "And these aren't sheep," she said, grinning. "Mother cows like to work down a hill, not up a mountain like sheep, so you want to stay on the downhill side when you're trailing them."

We helped Stan and Mary move cattle on the mountain all summer and fall. As soon as the snow fell, Mike gave me a rope and said, "Practice and be ready to rope in the branding corral by spring."

I roped everything in my house: chairs, tables, boots, water glasses. I learned to make coils, shake out a loop, jerk my slack, take my dallies—a half hitch around the saddle horn. The first branding was in April. I arrived with two horses, and Mike said, "You're up first." I looked at the corral full of cows and calves and all the young men in their twenties, including her son, Mart, with ropes in their hands and chew under their lips, watching my every move. "I can't go in there alone," I protested. "All I've roped is chairs!" She gave me no choice. Mart opened the gate and in I rode.

They were small calves bunched tightly enough in the corral so I could get to them, but not so crowded that my loop bumped into other cows. I made a big loop and threw it out. "Don't throw it like it was a sack of dirty laundry," Mart yelled, laughing. After the third try, two heels went into the loop. "Take your goddamned dallies," Mart yelled again. My hand, full of rope, went to the saddle horn. Caught. "Powder River!" Mike yelled out.

I dragged the calf to the branding fire. Then Mart rode in and joined me. For half an hour we roped together. He caught one and by the time it was vaccinated and branded, I had a calf waiting. To catch calf after calf was intoxicating. That first morning of roping, I couldn't miss. I was charmed—just that one time. Beginner's luck. Never to happen again.

When I rode out of the corral, Mike beamed a smile up at me, but said nothing. That year we cowboyed for the same two ranches and added one. We rode the fall roundup in the Wolf Mountains of southeastern Montana for a month. On the east slope of the Big Horns, we rode 150,000 acres of rolling hills and draws chock-full of wild plum trees.

Whenever we traveled to a ranch, I drove, pulling a six-horse trailer. On our way to one ranch we'd had three flat tires while crossing the mountains. We unloaded the horses, tied them to trees, unhooked the trailer, blocked the tires with a log, and drove back down to the valley for new tires. In Montana we took a short-cut through a highway construction zone. Halfway through, we almost tipped over. The pickup rocked so steeply to one side that the battery fell over and caught fire. I jumped out to turn our six horses loose, but the latch on the horse trailer was jammed. A truckload of Crow Indians drove by. I waved frantically but they just grinned and kept going. Mike raised the hood of the pickup and I grabbed a saddle pad, and together we smothered the fire. Finally we pried the back of the horse trailer open. We saddled two horses, led the others, and rode the last fifteen miles to the ranch.

The ranch rules were strict: breakfast at 3:30 A.M., saddle up by

4:15. Every morning we rode out in the dark. There were twelve riders, all men except us. The ground was frost-covered, and during the first few miles, the young horses always wanted to buck. By first light we could see the cattle far ahead. By the time the sun came over the ridge to the east, we had started gathering cattle. There was no lunch. At noon we had strung the gather—the cattle we were rounding up—out as far as the eye could see and were headed for home.

By 1:30 we were usually at the sorting corrals. We changed to fresh horses and sorted cattle in the corrals as three brand inspectors read every brand and we loaded them into waiting semis. By 3:00 P.M. we were finished. Dinner was at 4:00 and bed was soon after.

Except for the night we went to Harding to go dancing. The bars could be a little rough, but we soon ran into Charlie Secrest, a well-known horseman who would be riding with us the next day. Mike danced beautifully. She transformed the ugliest bar scene into a cotillion, sliding across the floor in polished boots, fresh Levi's, and red lipstick. We took turns dancing with Charlie until the band quit at 2:00 A.M., then drove to his ranch, picked up his two horses, and arrived back just in time to saddle up at 4:00. Northern lights were strobing vertically in the sky.

By the end of the first week we had all been bucked a few times. One of Mike's horses, Son, bucked me off twice before I even got my offside foot all the way over his back into the stirrup. The first time it happened we were still in the corral. He bucked, and I kicked out of the stirrups and flew off over his rump, landing on my feet. I was as surprised as everyone else. They gave me a round of applause.

When I looked around, adjusting my hat, Mike was standing behind me holding the horse's reins. "I'll hold him. You get on,"

she whispered. Always an ally, always trying to make me look better than I really was in front of the men. As I stepped on, the horse
bucked in place. Charlie Secrest rode over, grabbed the halter rope,
tied it to his saddle horn, snubbing me up to his horse. Son bucked
and bucked. It was like riding a rocking horse. Later Mike rode up
alongside me and said, "I guess he just doesn't like you." I never
had to ride Son again that year.

Mike and her husband, Frank, lived on a small ranch down the
mountain from ours. One winter she called and confessed that she
had cabin fever. "I think it's time to take a little tour," she said. As
usual, I was the driver. Up the mountain we went. There was a
roadblock at the top. The highway over to Sheridan was drifted in
and hadn't yet been plowed. "Oh what the hell, let's go anyway,"
Mike said, always a sport, and as my pickup broke through the first
drift, she yelled, "Powder River!"

At the Elks Club that night, her old cowboying buddies from the
Powder River drainage gathered around. A respected cowboy,
Mike was the center of attention. She had soft, pale blue eyes, rosy
cheeks, long legs, and a dry wit. Afterward we took a motel room
for a couple of days and went visiting. Storytelling all day, drinks,
steaks, and dancing at night. When she'd had enough, we drove
home.

Much of the history of Wyoming and Montana comes directly
from Texas. "They were poor but they knew how to handle a horse
and they always packed a few running irons—branding irons with
which you could change someone else's brand and make it your
own." Mike's grandfather, John Tisdale, was shot in the back in a
gulch outside Kaycee—an incident that precipitated the Johnson
County Cattle War. "He was coming back to the 3T with a buggy

load of Christmas presents and a new puppy for me. Frank Canton shot him in the back, unhitched the horses, and shot the dog too. It was cold-blooded murder. The rich ranchers had hired Canton to do it. They wanted all the land for themselves. They didn't want any of the smaller outfits to survive."

On our way out of town Mike asked me to pull into the cemetery. We walked through the graves: her grandfather's, then Nate Champion's—"one of the best cowboys ever," she said, then her mother's and father's. On the other side of the road we came to a stone that read FRANK CANTON. Mike pulled down her jeans and peed on his grave.

The next summer Mike and I merged our herds of cattle and continued to cowboy for all the neighbors. Her son and I went out together for a while, despite our ten-year age difference. Though his name is Mart, for Martin Alison, one of the rustling relatives, I called him "Martini, the Mad Man." That winter he called me from jail one night, after shooting a road sign from his pickup, almost killing the cop who was parked behind the sign. When I offered to bail him out, he said, "Oh that's okay. I like the TV dinners, and the stories you hear around here are pretty good."

When Mart and I were no longer together, I was still at Mike's house much of the time. In the spring we rode colts together. I would ride any horse in her presence because she never let me get into trouble I couldn't get out of. If a young horse started to act up, she was there, riding alongside, giving instruction and moral support.

Summers, when I was alone at my ranch from July to November, she made me leave a note on the table saying where I had ridden, and every evening she called to see if I was alive. Her loyalty in friendship was unparalleled. Once you were her friend, there was no turning back.

One winter Mike started having health problems. She was almost sixty. First breast cancer, then a heart attack. She hated hospitals, doctors, and the prospect of being in any way debilitated. She began, horror of horrors, walking. This for a woman whose motto was "If it can't be done horseback, it ain't worth doing." She thrived. But a second heart attack came a few years later, and she didn't phone the hospital soon enough. By the time she got to town, irreparable damage had been done to her heart muscle.

I was at the ranch by myself and our road was bad. When I got the news I had to walk out to the pickup parked on the paved road ten miles down the mountain. I drove to the hospital, sat on her bed, and talked. "Can't you sneak me a cigarette?" she asked. I shook my head no. Anything but that, I said. A drink, a steak . . . I'll walk your horse into the hospital. But not a cigarette. She smiled. She asked how my marriage was. I shrugged. She believed in manners and chivalry and didn't think my husband treated me well enough. "Women don't want to be treated like men," she said. "We should always be treated with respect. We just don't want to be left out, and there's no reason we should be. Riding with the men doesn't mean you have to become one." She looked at me, and whispered, "Don't let the bastards get you down." Meaning men.

Her eyelids drooped. She said she wanted to sleep. I promised to come back in the morning. As I started for the door, her pale eyes suddenly brightened: "Powder River, let her rip," she said, smiling. She died near dawn before I could see her again.

CIRCLING OTSEGO LAKE

• •

Diane Ackerman

In the lavender hours after daybreak, before the sun leapt onto the blue stage of the sky to begin its light opera of soul-searing heat, we set out on our bikes to circumnavigate Otsego Lake, which, encircled by dense forest, lay flat as pounded metal, thickly gray-purple with a light mist rising, yet wavering clear like an ancient mirror—the lake the Indians named "Glimmerglass"—and we pedaled hard up a long steep incline, as the temperature of our bodies and the day rose together, and within the aubergine drapery of the forest, twigs crackled, a confetti of light fell through the leaves, small quick beings darted among the tree trunks, and an occasional loud crunch or scuffling led our eyes back a million years through several tunnels of instinct to shadows we automatically interrogated for bear or mountain lion or highwayman or warrior, as a mixed chorus of insects and birds sang out, oblivious to our cycles, but mystified perhaps by our talk and laughter, or by the sight of a woman with blond hair riding upon a teal-green bike, wearing black shorts with purple chevrons the color of a mallard duck's underfeathers, and behind her the same thing but different—a woman with black hair riding upon a plum-colored bike—following a road dusted with loose gravel spread in winters past, weaving along undulating mountains that roll the way a dancer rolls her hips as she sprawls, while shadows staggered like eighth notes through the woods, the lake grew calm as cold wax, but the sun yellowed and swelled, and water began to seep from our faces, so we drank long gulps of clear warm water from bottles, not the lake water, deepening to black orchid whenever a castle-sized cloud drifted over, not the mirage of water shivering on baked macadam up ahead, not the salt water plumping up our cells that gives us shape and flow and spirits the mind through soul journeys, but water captured from a spring in Vermont we had never seen, filtered by rocks, as we are filtered by the sights we see, especially the majestic indigo of the lake, the lavender air, and the night purple convalescing in the forest, as we pedaled into the open where rich growing fields surrender to the sky their perfectly ordered rows of corn, with leaves like ironed green collars and tassels shaking glitter in the uproaring sun—sights we sometimes savored with little comment and a few delicate sips of mind, while at other times we wolfed down whole vistas. But we both knew the tonic value of the journey, which fell somewhere between pleasure and hardship, though we are not the sort of people who picnic on pain, or calibrate fun, but we reveled in working ourselves through the landscape, which we discovered tree by tree, farm mile by farm mile, with chicory and Queen Anne's lace bunching in the culverts, pedaling hard though we were steeped in pure exhaustion, pure exhilaration, leading us through the hinterlands where all emotional battles meet and become one tenderness, knowing that faraway behind us in the village of Cooperstown, shops would soon be lifting their awnings, museum doors yawning wide, and the great ladle of enterprise slowly stirring, as the sun rose higher and the town thrummed with a million colorful intrigues, but we were panting and pushing and pedaling and steadily pulling the day up behind us, changing gears, as sunballs of blinding neon raced over the lake, more violet than wet, and we biked toward noon, not thinking of showers, or rest, or grilled orange roughy served on a lakeside veranda where we would later stare in amazement at the lake we'd circled, stretching bright as a spill of mercury under the steadfast sun, but happily lost in a long serenade of mauve water, and the what-will-be somewhere around the bend.

BIOGRAPHICAL NOTES

••

DIANE ACKERMAN is the author of sixteen books about nature and human nature, including most recently *I Praise My Destroyer* (poetry) and *Deep Play* (nonfiction). The excerpt included in this anthology is from her memoir, *A Slender Thread*.

LEA ASCHKENAS is a staff writer with a weekly newspaper in San Luis Obispo, California. Her work has been published in *Salon, Outside*, the *San Francisco Bay Guardian, bike*, and *Beneath the Sleeping Maiden: Poets of Marin*. She is currently working on a collection of travel stories.

LUCY JANE BLEDSOE is the author of the novel *Working Parts*, winner of the 1998 American Librarian Association Gay/Lesbian/ Bisexual Award for Literature; of *Sweat: Stories and a Novella*; and of two novels for young people, *Tracks in the Snow* and *The Big Bike Race*. She is the editor of two collections of travel writing, *Gay Travels* and *Lesbian Travels*.

SARA CORBETT lives in Maine and writes frequently for a number of national magazines, including *Outside, Mirabella,* and *Esquire.* Her book, *Venus to the Hoop: A Gold Medal Year in Women's Basketball,* was published by Doubleday in 1997.

Born in Santa Barbara, California, GRETEL EHRLICH moved to Wyoming in 1976 where she ranched for 17 years. Her books include the nonfiction works: *The Solace of Open Spaces; Islands, The Universe, Home; A Match to the Heart; Yellowstone; Questions of Heaven,* and *Any Clear Thing That Blinds Us with Surprise,* as well as three collections of poetry, a novel, and a collection of short stories. She has received numerous awards including an NEA Creative Writing Fellowship, a Whiting Foundation Award, and a Guggenheim Fellowship. The American Academy of Arts and Letters honored her with the Harold B. Vurcell Award for distinguished prose in 1986. She divides her time between the central coast of California and Wyoming.

JEAN GOULD is the author of a novel, *Divorcing Your Grandmother,* and the editor of *Season of Adventure: Traveling Tales and Outdoor Journeys by Women over Fifty* and *Dutiful Daughters: Caring for Our Parents as They Grow Old.* Other essays about the Himalaya have been published in *Another Wilderness, Maiden Voyages,* and *Sojourner.* Currently she is a visiting scholar in women's studies at Northeastern University.

PAM HOUSTON's collection of short stories, *Cowboys Are My Weakness,* was a winner of the 1993 Western States Book Award and has been translated into nine languages. She has edited a collection titled *Women on Hunting.* Stories from her second collection of fiction, *Waltzing the Cat,* were chosen for both the 1998 Best American Short Stories and the O'Henry Awards. Her first essay collection, *A Little More About Me,* which includes "Breaking the Ice," was published in September 1999. Houston is a licensed river guide and a horsewoman who teaches in the MFA program at the University of California, Davis. From time to time she appears on *CBS Sunday Morning* doing literary essays on the wilderness. She lives in Colorado at 9,000 feet near the headwaters of the Rio Grande.

AMY IRVINE lives in Salt Lake City, Utah, where she works as a freelance writer and as a grant writer for a grassroots environmental organization working to protect Utah wilderness. She has rock climbed for twelve years and taught climbing clinics for women around the country.

B K LOREN's work has been published in places like *Orion* and *Talking River Review.* She was this year's recipient of the Mary Roberts Rinehart National Creative Nonfiction Award and is currently at work on several long writing projects.

KATHLEEN DEAN MOORE is the chair of the Department of Philosophy at Oregon State University and an essayist whose work has appeared in *The New York Times Magazine, North American Review, Field and Stream,* and other places. She is author of a collection of nature essays, *Riverwalking: Reflections on Moving Water,* which won the Pacific Northwest Bookseller's 1996 Book Award, and a second collection of essays, *Holdfast: At Home in the Natural World.*

HOLLY MORRIS is the editor of *A Different Angle: Fly-Fishing Stories by Women* and *Uncommon Waters: Women Write about Fishing.* Her writing has appeared in several literary anthologies, as well as in ABCNEWS.com and *The New York Times Book Review*. She is the creator and host of the television documentary series *Adventure Divas*. She lives in Seattle.

MARY MORRIS is the author of ten books, including four novels, three collections of short stories, and a trilogy of travel memoirs, including *Nothing to Declare: Memoirs of a Woman Traveling Alone*. She has also coedited with her husband, Larry O'Connor, *Maiden Voyages*, an anthology of the travel literature of women. Her numerous short stories and essays have appeared in such places as *The Paris Review, The New York Times*, and *Vogue*. The recipient of a Guggenheim and the Rome Prize in Literature from the American Academy of Arts and Letters, Morris teaches writing at Sarah Lawrence College and lives in Brooklyn with her husband and twelve-year-old daughter.

HANNAH NYALA'S first book, *Point Last Seen: A Woman Tracker's Story*, was made into a CBS movie starring Linda Hamilton and is now being developed for a one-hour drama series for television. She is currently finishing her second book, *Walking Blind: A Tracker's Journey to the Snowline in the Kalahari,* and her first novel, *Will's War.* Hannah has M.A. degrees in history and anthropology and still labors under the illusion that someday she might actually finish her Ph.D. in colonial U.S. history (UW-Madison). She lives in a tiny house in a tiny midwestern village, and keeps herself from having an empty nest by filling it with lots of animals and plants.

LISA PRICE, originally from Pottsville, Pennsylvania, is a freelance writer who moved to Maine shortly after completing her

Appalachian Trail hike. She is a columnist for *The Maine Sportsman* and *Bow & Arrow Hunting* magazines, in addition to writing for various outdoor publications.

BRIDGET QUINN grew up in Great Falls, Montana, and now lives and writes in San Francisco, California. She has published essays in *Solo: On Her Own Adventure, Mademoiselle,* and *SWING,* and short stories in *Thema, So To Speak,* and *ELF: Eclectic Literary Forum.* She recently finished her first novel.

KIM TODD recently received an M.F.A. in creative writing from the University of Montana. Her essays and articles have appeared in *Orion, Backpacker, The Bellingham Review,* and *Cutbank.*

ALSO AVAILABLE FROM VINTAGE BOOKS

THE ROAD FROM COORAIN
by Jill Ker Conway

A remarkable woman's clear-sighted memoir of growing up Australian; from the vastness of a sheep station in the outback to the stifling propriety of postwar Sydney; from an untutored childhood to a life in academia; and from the shelter of a protective family to the lessons of independence.

Autobiography/0-679-72436-2

SHOOTING THE BOH
A Woman's Voyage Down the Wildest River in Borneo
by Tracy Johnston

When Tracy Johnston signed up for a rafting expedition down Borneo's Boh River, she had no idea that it had never been fully navigated, nor did she know about the local wildlife, which included swimming cobras and swarms of sweat-eating bees. But perhaps the most revealing discovery was what she learned about herself: about what it means to be an adventurer—a woman adventurer—in a world that seems to be made exclusively for the young.

Travel/Adventure/0-679-74010-4

MAIDEN VOYAGES
Writings of Women Travelers
edited and with an Introduction by Mary Morris

Whether it is Edith Wharton, marveling at the magical beauty of a Marrakech palace garden, or Mildred Cable, wondering at dust demons and phantom voices in the Gobi Desert, the women gathered in this generous and delightful anthology show as much of themselves as they show of the strange and wonderful places they visit.

Travel/Women's Studies/0-679-74030-9

VINTAGE DEPARTURES
Available from your local bookstore, or call toll-free to order:
1-800-793-2665 (credit cards only).